I CHING
DIVINATION
for today's woman

I CHING DIVINATION
for today's woman

by

Cassandra Eason

foulsham
London • New York • Toronto • Sydney

foulsham
Yeovil Road, Slough, Berkshire, SL1 4JH

ISBN 0-572-01895-9

Copyright © 1994 Cassandra Eason

Phototypeset in Great Britain by Typesetting Solutions,
Slough, Berkshire.
Printed in Great Britian by Cox & Wyman Ltd.,
Reading, Berkshire

I CHING DIVINATION
for today's woman

CONTENTS

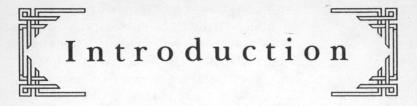

Introduction

Confucius declared, at a great age, that if he had another 70 years of life he would devote 50 of them to the study of the *I Ching, The Book of Changes,* the great Chinese oracle. Mrs Confucius must have raised her eyes to the great Dragon in the sky at the prospect of even another hour of listening to such male outpourings as:

'She must not follow her whims. She must attend within to the food. As a King he approaches his family. Fear not'.
(from Hexagram 37 Chia Jen – the Family.)

History tells us next to nothing about Mrs Confucius — we know she existed because Confucius had children. We can only imagine her, bustling about the house as her learned husband spent hours contemplating the oracle by a complicated ritual involving passing bundles of yarrow stalks from hand to hand, then drawing diagrams and consulting an ancient tome. We can guess who had to sweep up all those scattered yarrow stalks afterwards — the Chinese character for wife is a symbolic representation of a woman with a broom in her hand.

At first sight it seems the *I Ching* has little to offer women. But can we afford to cast off something that is central to Chinese philosophy, and is regarded as a source of wisdom in the same way as the Western world regards the Bible? Firstly, how do you pronounce *I Ching?* You can say *eye jing,* although some pronounce it *ee jeng.* Use whichever you prefer and ignore the 'Oriental experts' who crop up in every wine bar and launderette with their pocket guides. Or you may prefer the 'say-as-you-see' version *eye ching* that most people use.

The experts have been around for a long time, ever since the *I Ching* first cropped up before 5000 BC. For many years it was not written down. It is thought that it was first recorded in about 1700 BC when it still retained a very simple form.

King Wen and his son, the Duke of Chou, greatly expanded the explanations round about 1132 BC. So Confucius was a comparative newcomer when he or his followers added yet more interpretations in the sixth century BC.

Many people do devote a lifetime of study to the intellectual wealth of the ages, though many are put off by the vast amount of overlaying ritual and so ignore a system that, at heart, is as simple and yet as complex as life itself. Casting the oracle usually involves highly complex ritual calculations during a period of meditation. This is followed by references to a vast book which has been highly biased towards the male. It contains lots of useful warnings about the dangers involved in marrying a maiden, and advice on how to treat a concubine, but bears about as much relevance to the life of a modern woman as a civil service manual (in fact, the people who put together the commentaries on the *I Ching* regarded the civil service as the highest possible profession).

So why bother with this ancient form of divination? I became interested when I started thinking about the title: *the Book of Changes.* For a woman's life is all about change, far more so than a man's.

We've all met those men in their 80s, schoolboys still, unscathed by passing through careers, wars, marriage, births and deaths. But a woman must make so many changes. When it comes to marriage it is not just our names we change, but also our natures; for even in these liberated days, some women still accept the role of the lesser partner who 'must follow her husband'.

The change to motherhood is even more drastic for, more often than not, we are the nurturers — there are still men today who go through life with little more involvement with their offspring than they have with casual acquaintances at work.

When the children flee the nest, life changes again for the woman, while many a man continues in his chosen career as though nothing has happened. And in a way it hasn't — to him.

If a woman decides not to have children she must consider the consequences of such a drastic change from the normally accepted lifestyle. For us the biological clock is ticking away: from the first period to the Big Change we are constantly under pressure.

The Chinese believed that the *I Ching* could predict such changes and could offer advice on which path to take. This seemed invaluable to women, so I began looking back at the essentials of the system and found it was gloriously simple, once stripped of the complications imposed upon it by the men of the Chinese Civil Service. At its roots, the *I Ching* relies on drawing from the well of our unconscious intuition answers to the questions that trouble people of all ages and cultures. Most importantly, it can tap that deep-set, inner knowledge that women use every day of their lives.

The thoughts of Mrs Confucius or the Empress Wen, unlike their more esteemed male counterparts who helped to give a male-bias to the *I Ching*, are not recorded for posterity, but there must have been many women, thousands of years ago, who were not that keen on the 'Have my slippers and rice bowl waiting and the bed warm when I come back from the hill of contemplation, dear,' approach. We may no longer bind our feet to please our masters, but more subtle constraints still conspire to keep a woman hard at it, combining career and home and trying to make time for her own needs.

So what is the *I Ching?* At heart it consists of 64 basic answers that apply to the many different questions you may ask. The answers definitely work as I've discovered in hundreds of readings for myself and other people. But these answers aren't really 64 separate ideas at all. They are built up round eight basic elements that you are already familiar with such as water (going with the flow) and thunder (shaking things up a bit). These you can combine yourself in a remarkably common-sense way to reach the inner wisdom of the *I Ching,* thereby cutting about 359 pages from the size of the average *I Ching* book. In fact, once you have learned this system you can leave my book behind.

But this book isn't selling you short. Indeed this method will actually help you to understand and use the full *I Ching* method yourself after only a few days, and you won't be tied to other people's interpretations. No hefty expensive volumes to weigh you down, just you, your little bag of *I Ching* stones that we are going to make, and your life stretching before you.

The underlying principle of the *I Ching* is that of *yang* and *yin. Yang* corresponds roughly to positive, male, light, creative — you know the usual macho male attributes, and *yin* to negative, female, dark, receptive — yes, good, old Mrs Confucius no less, with broom in hand, sweeping up the cast-off prophecies. The female is often seen as a marc or a big old cart that carries everything — man saved the dragon image for himself. But *yang* and *yin* are, in the *I Ching* as in life, equally essential for the turning of the world, and each contains bits of the other and can change rapidly into the other. Jung had the same idea, that the male has a caring, gentle side (his *anima*) and the female a dynamic, thrusting side (her *animus*) that are essential for a well-balanced personality. Not surprisingly Jung was an *I Ching* addict. As for the positive and negative aspects, it's not in the 'yes' and 'no', 'right' and 'wrong' sense, but more like electricity, where the positive charge is useless without the negative pole.

The point of the *I Ching* system is that it doesn't say our future is fixed, but that our reactions to change can determine our own futures. Change equals adapting to situations, making do and mending, knowing when to look rather than leap, and when to accept the way things are rather than rush in, all guns blazing. And, of course, there is a point when it's time to turn your back on the washing up and head for the sunrise. No wonder the ancients had to hide this exciting form of divination from women. The women of Ancient China, or even Victorian England for that matter, would have been throwing their rice bowls or smelling salts over the windmill in their thousands.

For, as I have already said, using one's inner intuitions (dipping deep into the *I Ching*) is what women have for centuries based their 'magic' on, and so we're three-quarters of the way there before we've drawn our first *yin* line.

So how do we find out which answer applies to us at a particular time? The guys, having all the time in the world, devised an incredibly complex and hour-long system with yarrow stalks. Basically the idea of taking an age about the *I Ching* was to give men the time and space to get in touch with their unconscious — something generally harder for men then as now because of society's conditioning. (Men are, perhaps unfairly, too often still expected to be down-to-earth and practical.) Others tried to speed things up a little by throwing coins and doing complicated sums on bits of paper (like a Chinese times-table). Then came the really complicated bit, reading out incomprehensible mottoes about superior men and marrying maidens scuttling ten paces behind, struggling under a load of used yarrow stalks. Then, at long last, comes the reason you consulted the *I Ching* in the first place — it shows you how to apply the answer it gives to the present problem, assuming you haven't forgotten the original question or gone to make the tea.

But this may be where your problems start. What can some obscure line reveal about your middle-aged spread, or overdrawn bank balance, or the guy in the office whose only interest in statistics is your vital ones?

To give an example of the problem — how about an extract from the change lines of *Hexagram 54 The Marrying Maiden — Kuei Mei:*

'The marrying maiden as a slave,
She marries as a concubine'.

The interpretation in a very esteemed translation is: 'A girl who is in a lowly position and finds no husband may, in some circumstances, still win a place as a concubine.'

Now the question you were asking was, 'what can I do about my adolescent son who has doubled my electricity bill with his bank of electronic computers, television and stereo blaring day and night and obsession for tumble-dried jeans?' OK, you feel like a slave, but the hexagram seems to be saying, make the best of it, mum — maybe you could get a night job as well to keep the young master happy.

But let's look at the image of the hexagram, a Lake with Thunder over it. Your son is all tranquillity, but you're absorbing the tensions yourself. So let the old thunder rip, and ruffle his surface a bit — how about billing him for a bit of that electricity or even putting him on a separate meter?

So let's head straight for the spirit of the *I Ching,* which, unlike the previous pearls of wisdom, is as fresh and relevant today as it was when it was written for a social system where the ultimate Mr Cool, pictured naturally with his head sticking through the clouds, was a glorified inspector of taxes.

All you need are a set of flat pebbles from the park or beach and a felt tip pen.

By writing our *yang* (unbroken lines) and *yin* (broken lines) on these stones, we can then actually find our answers with no brain-twisting calculations.

We'll learn the eight basic ideas first and see what they mean in modern and female terms. Then we can practise combining them and see how one situation influences another.

And the magic? By random selection of the stones out of a bag, the answers that emerge, even to our unformulated queries, will have tapped the deep well of feminine power.

Can the *I Ching* really be that simple? Yes, if we keep the essence and cut through the window dressing. For if, as women, we're going to have it all: career, family and fulfilment, we've got to run twice as hard and three times as fast as the men. While our mighty hunters are keeping a weather eye for potential concubines on the 17.22 from Waterloo to Woking, the *Woman's I Ching* uses the back door to enlightenment. By tapping into our personal magic, using the insights that were there 3,000 years ago, we can use the *I Ching* to illuminate our lives.

The *I Ching, the Book of Changes,* has, by its very name, the capacity to adapt to the changing modern world where women are carving out a place for themselves, and, hopefully, we can take the men with us, and put down our symbolic broom.

Using I Ching

We'll start by looking at the basics. Here is an example of the oracle.

Your first thought may be: 'What on earth can these lines mean to me?' My first reaction was to reach for a bottle of wine and the newspaper to see if there was anything worth watching on television. But don't panic — all will become clear if we take it in careful stages.

This is a hexagram, so called because it is made up of six lines and is the basis for *I Ching* divination. In fact, it is the Thunder/Lake hexagram, called traditionally *Sui* which means 'following'. As you can see, it is made up of broken and unbroken lines. These represent the elements *yang* and *yin* which we met in the introduction.

Yang, shown by an unbroken line, represents the creative, logical and assertive element in our lives, and is an essential part of a woman's make-up if she is not to be swamped by the needs of others.

Trigrams and hexagrams

Yang, *shown by an unbroken line* _____

Yin, *shown by a broken line* ____ ____

Yin, shown by a broken line, is the receptive, accepting, intuitive side that is integral to being a woman. But it is also important for a man to acknowledge his gentler side.

The basis of the *I Ching* is the way these two elements combine or oppose each other in the hexagram. This can tell us how our life is unfolding and what the possibilities are. It sounds far more complicated than it is. We shall break it down into easy stages by first learning what are called the trigrams, that is the three vertical lines of *yangs* and *yins* that make up each of the eight elements; and it's pretty self-evident that our Thunder/Lake hexagram is simply two trigrams put together.

How do we create trigrams and hexagrams? First by dispensing with the complicated rituals. We are going to make *Ching* stones, which will have a *yang* on one side and a *yin* on the other. By choosing three of these at random we will create our trigram.

The only thing to remember is that in this system you read from the bottom line upwards, so the top line is the last stone you put down and read.

Day
2

Making the Stones

To make the first set of *Ching* stones, find six flat pebbles the size of a 2p piece at least and get a felt tip pen — a water-resistant one is best in case the stones get wet. (After all, someone you read for might burst into tears of gratitude).

If you can't get any suitable stones then wooden draughts will do. In fact, you can use anything of that size and rough shape. Now simply mark each of the six 'stones' with a broken line *(yin)* on one side and an unbroken line *(yang)* on the other. We are going to use these instead of those complicated yarrow stalks, fiddly coins, and elusive pen and paper that are never around when needed.

You then need something to keep your stones in — a little drawstring bag or purse, big enough to hold eventually the six stones. The important thing is to be able to take the stones out at random without seeing which surface is uppermost.

The Sky trigram

There are eight basic trigrams and these represent what the ancients considered to be the basic elements that made up life. Modern physics has made this much more complicated, but we do not need an atomic table of the elements because we are sticking to the old ideas.

Here for a start is **Sky**.

This is formed when three of the Ching stones you have drawn from the bag are three *yangs* — the unbroken lines.

Yang is the positive element, so the message from the Sky trigram is one of get-up-and-go. If you make this trigram then, the sky's the limit right now. You know that your energy level is pretty high and you're heading for the winning post. You'll be using your head rather than your heart and you are putting yourself first rather than coming a poor second to everyone else. This is a conscious, not unconscious stage in your life, relying on a definite choice, not intuition.

Yang *is the positive element*

Such deliberate positive action once in a while is no bad thing, because women often tend not to think of their ultimate destination. It's still the boys who make the first dash to use the computers, and even the most liberated partner may look in amazement if the woman suggests that he takes time off to transport a sick relative to the doctor — even if it's his own mother.

Later on when we meet the hexagrams, (two trigrams, one on top of the other) you'll sometimes get six unbroken (*yang*) lines: the Double Dragon is a double dose of the creative energy. So it really is the time to get up and go for it.

The only problem with the pure Sky trigram is that we can end up trying to be more macho than the men and then we ignore all those lovely intuitive parts of our nature that can give us the edge in business as well as in the home.

So how does the Sky trigram fit in with modern everyday life? Let's look at the case of Pam.

Pam's story

Pam is in her early 30s and came to my first *I Ching* class with her mother. She lives at home and suffers from dreadful, regular migraines. She'd got a chance to join the Forces and had passed the medical, but Mum said that with her migraines the strain would be too much. Pam turned over first a *yang* (at the bottom), then another *yang* and finally a third to put on top. Even without knowing the three yangs stood for Sky, Pam could see that the lines were saying that she should go for it and make her own mark in the world. At that time she was absorbing Mum's negative vibes, so a very important part of herself, the desire for independence and personal achievement, was being drained away.

Day 4

The Earth trigram

The **Earth** has three broken *yin* lines.

This is seen as the basic female trigram element and is the seat of intuition, buried deep in the unconscious, the world of instinctive rather than conscious thought, the ability to sum someone up in five seconds flat, or know when a child or partner is in danger. Accepting unconditionally rather than criticising others, listening rather than talking, nurturing rather than demanding can be enormously creative and satisfying. Here, woman is central in her role as healer and reconciler, whether within the family or the world of work. But the caring message of the Earth trigram is not indicating the road to being resident doormat or martyr. Caring for ourselves is integral in this element, accepting our own weaknesses and darker side as well as forgiving others. We do all get angry, jealous, resentful, and so it's wasting vital energy trying to be ever-smiling and patient instead of looking for our own needs to be met.

Earth

Sometimes when you meet the hexagrams (six lines) you'll get six broken *yin* lines and you'll know that it's not a time to go off on your own, as your role is pretty vital to other people right now.

The only problem with pure Earth is that we can get a bit swamped with the Mother Earth tag and lose our unique identity.

What does the Earth trigram say to the modern woman?

Georgina's story

In contrast to Pam, Georgina, who was also in her 30s, was a mother of two young children. Unlike some women who do feel very frustrated staying at home as a full-time carer, Georgina was actually enjoying her time with the children and the opportunities it gave her for organising her own day. But friends with careers were pressuring her into feeling she'd opted out of the real world, and a chance had come to return to her old post as an executive officer in the civil service. Georgina pulled out first a *yin*. Her next stone, which she put above it, was another *yin* and the third was also a *yin*. So the *Ching* seemed to be answering her unvoiced question by saying: 'Listen to what you feel is right for you and not for others.'

The receptive, caring side of Georgina's nature was the one that was having an opportunity to develop and was giving an added dimension to her world. The stones reflected what deep down she wanted to do, as opposed to what other people said she ought to want, and so she decided to turn down the job.

The stones aren't casting a verdict that is true for all time — just what is right at this moment. Next month or next year Georgina's reading might show that she is ready to develop another facet of her nature.

People sometimes say: 'Why didn't the *Ching* tell me that last time?' The answer is that you were at a different stage then. You can't have a once-and-for-all reading, any more than you can say: 'Right, I've arrived, feet up all the way from now on.' Remember we are talking about *The Book of Changes*.

The first two trigrams can be considered as the 'all-the-same trigrams' all *yangs* or all *yins*. The 'sandwich' trigrams are equally easy to remember. Here you look at the line in the middle which is different from the two sandwiching it. These 'sandwich' trigrams are Fire and Water and since Fire is generally more dynamic than Water (think of lightning in the sky), its middle (the bit where the fuel comes) is sandwiched between two of those oomphy *yangs*. Or look at it another way. We can recognise fire because it flickers (broken line) between the lines of the grate.

The Fire trigram

Fire

Fire is two *yangs* sandwiching a *yin*. Though some *I Ching* books regard the trigrams in terms of family, e.g.: Fire is seen as the middle daughter because the *yin* is in the middle and is feminine. I find this a bit confusing and limiting, but do use this if you find it helpful.

In these trigrams, it is what is in the middle that gives us the clue as to what the trigram is. The fire is seen clinging, in the shape of the trigram, to whatever fuels it, for fire can't exist in isolation but needs to feed on something solid in order to burn. So fire is very much the element of communicating what has been absorbed, of destroying the old and unneeded and clearing the way for reconstruction or renewal. But you should only speak if you are sure of your facts or feelings, otherwise the initial spark can go out. It warms, illumines, provides the power for change, from raw into cooked; it forges things together in a new strong metallic form.

And so for women, after that initial Sky energy (and here we've still got two *yangs* to keep us going — the creative power), comes the next stage of creative endeavour. This gives the creativity a very real and solid basis for putting all those theories into workable practice, and turning all those inspirational dreams into reality. This is the trigram of the sun which tells you that you can fulfil all your potential even given your earthly constraints, whatever age you are.

Fire can be initiated naturally either from the sky as lightning or deep below the earth's crust, emerging as volcanoes.

The only danger with fire is that it might run out of fuel or that it will destroy the good with the bad.

If you get a double dose of fire in the six-line hexagram, then maybe it's time to speak your mind, or put into action that new plan at work.

What does this mean to the modern woman?

Esther's story

Esther is in her late 50s and has moved away from her family to a new part of the country, following the death of her husband. She had felt she didn't want to depend on her children, but wished to carry out the plans she had made with her husband before his unexpected death — to retire to their holiday cottage and take up her painting seriously. So Esther has had her Sky leap. However, she has recently started to wonder whether she has been over-hasty. This is the point where all that vibrant energy peters out, when it hits the first snag and you wish you hadn't bothered. Esther turns over first a *yang* (unbroken line) then a *yin* (broken) and finally a *yang* at the top.

The Fire trigram shows Esther that, having made the initial leap, now is the time to put all her ideas, and especially the creative ones, into practice. She has all the skills she learned in her painting classes to cling to and she can use them to forge perhaps a new career or at least a very absorbing interest. Her art is the communication of her inner resources and potential (the fire from within the earth). The situation is not ideal, alone without the partner she loved, but it is not a time to run back to the security of her family. Again her trigram may change but, for now, it's time to apply both the energy and her very solid abilities.

Day

6

The Water trigram

Water, the fourth trigram, is the other sandwich configuration, two receptive or broken lines sandwiching a *yang* — the continuous flow of the river within its banks. And here we've got the unbroken power of the *yang* moving forward, though the external circumstances (the banks or *yins*) may change. Here the middle *yang* tells us of the persistence of water and movement.

But the *yins* show that the water is sufficiently adaptable to fill available spaces, to go round obstacles, rather than burn them down as Fire does. 'Going with the flow' is a popular modern expression and that is what the Water trigram is all about. Of course, there are dangers inherent, and another description of this trigram is 'the Abyss': the only way forward is straight down the rushing waterfall. But sometimes, if there are rapids ahead, we just have to hang on to that canoe

Water

and hope for the best. This is not the planned leap of the Sky nor the application of skills as with Fire, but following life where it takes you and being prepared to try new ventures, if that is where the flow takes you. To me this is an exciting trigram. It's not one to indicate that you should sit at home with your feet up, but says it is time to get out your brolly and follow the unexplored path.

A double Water in the hexagram indicates you've been hesitating and agonising too long. Let go and let the boat take you where it will. The only problem with pure Water is that you often don't recognise when it's time to start paddling and controlling the direction.

Pauline's story

Pauline, who is divorced and in her 40s, was suddenly made redundant and, in spite of many job applications, seemed to be getting nowhere. Her nights were spent in lying awake brooding over the unfairness of the situation, and, though she could just about manage financially, she felt totally drained of any energy. So when a retraining place came up at a local college she felt it was totally pointless following this new path, since job opportunities were so few in her area.

Pauline drew first a *yin* (broken) line, then a *yang* (unbroken) and finally another *yin*. Though there's not a lot of directed energy around (only one *yang*) it is right in the middle, and so there is movement. The Water trigram suggests that instead of wasting energy by tossing and turning, Pauline should accept her situation and follow any opportunities that might offer themselves, however unlikely they may seem. The training place, although appearing to have no immediate advantage, could be an opening for the future. At any rate, it would get Pauline out of the stagnant pond of regrets she is in and start her moving again. And at the end of it she may see a job in another area (Pauline has no ties after all), but for now she should certainly go with the flow. She may be surprised where she ends up.

The Thunder trigram

The next two I call the 'bottom line' trigrams, and are those of movement. Most of us have a bottom line beyond which we cast off our intertia and peace-loving ways and instigate change. Since, in the *Ching*, everything moves from bottom to top, we need to look at the bottom line to tell us which of the two movement trigrams we have drawn.

Thunder is the trigram of sudden change.

Thunder

Think of it as the unbroken power rising upwards from the earth. The ancient idea was that the thunder came out of the earth in the spring and scattered the seeds of creation. Or, if you find it easier, think of the Thunder (single *yang* power) shattering the two sky lines. However you remember it, the appearance of Thunder is going to herald a deliberate decision for change in the status quo at any time of the year.

Thunder comes at the times when the woman has had enough and says, 'Right — on your bike' to unfaithful lover-boy, or announces to her comatose spouse, 'I'm going on that world cruise right now before I need my zimmer frame.'

For Thunder heralds the crunch time and comes from deep within a woman, temporarily displacing those nurturing *yins*. It's not always a life and death matter — maybe you've simply decided you're not working through your lunch-hour any more.

Thunder trigram states very clearly to those nearby what your limits are, which is where the *I Ching* idea of Thunder as shock comes in. It can be a shock both to the woman announcing the change and those around her. For the unwillingness to rock the boat, that had Mrs Noah mucking out the animals while Mr Noah and all those sons charted the course, goes overboard and everyone's swimming for shore.

So Thunder can be a very positive trigram for a woman in making sure she gets her bit of the cake or computer time. Thunder is often felt in the air when 'You don't mind, do you?' precedes one too many conversations in which the woman is going to be lumbered with yet another task. Double Thunder and the change is a big one.

The only drawback with Thunder is that it can lead to a lot of empty threats, and so people learn not to take your outbursts seriously. Be prepared to do what you say and save your Thunder for the big storms in life, not the passing showers.

Peggy's story

Peggy, a single parent, finally saw red when her son of 14, who demanded constant room service and communicated only in grunts, informed her that he wished to live his own life his own way without interference. She came home after a hard day at work to discover William had appropriated the family's television, as his was broken, leaving Peggy unable to watch her favourite soap opera.

Not surprisingly Peggy drew a *yang* (unbroken line), followed by two *yins* (broken lines). So Number One Son was in for a shock. Peggy didn't shout and rage but she determined on change. She found out the cost of renting a television and hired one, deducting half the rental (well, she was still his mother) from William's weekly allowance. And her son took his first step towards living his own life.

Trivial? Ninety-five per cent of our lives is made up of such trivial issues, and only if we can get our lives right at this level will we have the energy for touching the stars. The *I Ching* is equally effective whether the change is finding a new milkman or a new career.

Day

8

The Tree trigram

Tree, the trigram of more gradual change.

This is the other way of coping when we reach the bottom line of life. Because it is a trigram heralding movement, it is the single line at the bottom which we need to look at. The Tree trigram is made up of a *yin* at the bottom followed by two *yangs* above.

Tree

Think of it as the tree (the growing thing at the bottom) pushing its way upwards from the earth (broken line) to the sky (unbroken two lines). The traditional system is a bit confusing regarding this trigram, sometimes calling it wind and sometimes wood (referring to a tree). Which meaning you use in the old system depends on the hexagram it's in and whether there is an 'r' in the month. So I road-tested both definitions to see which was more relevant to today's woman.

Wind was a bit of a disaster. Images veered between gastric associations and Winnie the Pooh and the Blustery Day, and since the whole point of the trigram is that you aren't straw for any wind that blows, we ended up due east of Square One.

In contrast, Tree was an instant success and the idea came over of the tree growing (a gradual movement) and standing firm against disruption. So Tree it is, and it represents the more usual female way of progressing and instituting change an inch at a time, and pretty hard work it usually proves to be.

We've all heard of the glass ceiling that stops women getting to the top in business, and how many women have their personal inner growth stunted by the demands of others. Women are also subjected to the pressures of family and friends; this may start as love, but often ends in emotional blackmail unless you do state the bottom line of your tolerance. And then there's guilt. That's something every woman needs to stand firm against.

The double Tree image in the hexagram promises quiet persistence against a pretty hefty obstacle. The only problem with the Tree trigram is when the positive quality of persistence keeps a woman banging her head against a brick wall in what really is a hopeless situation. But then you find the Thunder turns up.

So where does that leave us today?

Gayle's story

Gayle, a widow, is 70 and doesn't want to be put out to grass. She has found things difficult to manage recently as she suffers from arthritis. Her married son Tim wants her to move into a residential home near him at the other end of the country, but Gayle is used to her independence and prefers to wait for a sheltered bungalow in her own area. Tim says it's unfair to make him worry about her welfare and she is getting worn down by his haranguing phone calls, though, in fact, she makes no demands on him.

Gayle draws first a *yin* (broken line) then two *yangs* (unbroken lines) above it. She found the Tree trigram summed up her feelings exactly, for she felt like a tree trying to stand firm while being buffeted by her physical difficulties and her son's emotional pressures. So should she uproot and move? After all, this is a trigram of movement.

We discussed the situation and decided 'No' because she would have been moving for her son's peace of mind not her own, and, even at 70, Gayle has plenty of growing and living still to do. She perhaps needs to persist in her own quiet way to get all the available help in her present situation, and to try to hasten her preferred move to sheltered accommodation in the area she knows and likes.

Day 9

The last two trigrams are the 'keeping the lid on' trigrams. They talk about stillness, and here we need to look at the top line to tell us whether it is an 'up there' sky stillness or a stillness dipping into the earth. The two are very different things.

The Mountain trigram

The **Mountain** has two lower *yins* (broken lines) and an unbroken *yang* on top. The earth (broken lines) has piled up to touch the sky (unbroken line).

Mountain

The top line or lid is in the sky and so you know this trigram is about sky stillness, the getting away from it all, (the usual male solution

to pressure is, not to take himself to the top of the mountain, but rather to the pub or the club to get away from his domestic pressures).

But if the woman opts out, it tends to be more of a mental process; though you may be tempted to go off to the nearest wine bar if the man in your life is having his dark night of the soul because his beloved motor bike has developed a terminal rattle. So, if a Mountain trigram appears, perhaps the answer lies in accepting that you cannot make all the people happy all of the time. Take any mother on an annual holiday, whether to Frinton or the Costa del Fritos, and she'll end up desperately trying to marry together sulky adolescents, complaining aunties, toddlers whining for an ice cream every five minutes, and a partner who has come to get away from it all and does just that. What is the woman's souvenir? — a migraine that lasts long after the donkey with the straw hat has disintegrated on the flight home.

Now the guy in the deck-chair had got it spot on with the Mountain bit, and so, with a bit of practice, can the woman. This involves not confronting anyone (as opposed to the Thunder trigram), but letting the rest of the world rush around like demented road runners for a change.

Many women, by acting as peace-makers and cheerleaders for humanity, place themselves in the firing line of what are really other people's quarrels, and so end up unconsciously giving the combatants the audience they crave.

The chance of the average woman being able to take herself to the top of a mountain, or even to a meditation seminar, is a bit remote (for many of us five minutes peace in the loo would be bliss). But we can opt out of what is not our responsibility and define what our own boundaries are.

A double Mountain in the hexagram and it's time to plug your ears with cotton wool, and go for a walk at lunch-time, if the office politics are getting a bit too serious. The role of the mediator and bearer of bad tidings is no happier today than it was in the Ancient Greek world, when messengers could be killed for bringing unwanted news. So, step out of the firing line and watch the arrows fly overhead.

The only danger with pure Mountain is you can forget to come down again. This is unlikely, with those nearest to you banging on the bathroom door of life.

June's story

June is in her early 20s and finds herself in the middle of a feud at the bank where she works. Jenny, a new assistant manager, has been brought in over the head of June's friend, Gill, who is in her 30s and was hoping for a high-flying career. Gill makes it extremely hard for the newcomer because she won't offer any information or help, unless forced to do so. In return, Jenny criticises Gill at every count. Gill naturally bends June's ear as often as possible and sees June's cooperation with her superior as disloyalty. However, June has to act as secretary to the new assistant manager and finds that, except on the issue of Gill, Jenny is easy to get along with. Recently Jenny has been trying to get June to side with her, and June ends up carrying snide comments and notes between the two. In a recent confrontation, June found herself in the middle and getting flak from both sides. June draws two *yins* (broken lines) followed by a *yang* on top.

The Mountain trigram reflects June's longing to sit on top of a mountain away from it all. And that's just what she should do, though it's not easy in practice, especially if, as with June, you want a happy atmosphere at work. Mountains may be in short supply in Basildon High Street, but June can take herself up and away by other means.

First, she needs to stop acting as go-between (remember the swift and untimely demise of the Greek messengers). It is not part of June's official brief to carry bitchy tidings, and she must tell Gill that although they are friends, she cannot act as an intermediary in this way at work, nor can she go against the boss at a professional level. Secondly, she has to explain to Jenny that she can't and won't take sides over a personality clash, and that the battle is strictly between Gill and Jenny. June can be pleasant to both combatants but she does need to distance herself, and maybe go window-shopping at lunchtime rather than feeding the lions at work. Who knows, without June taking the brunt of the aggro, the opponents may settle down and confine themselves to the odd hiss?

On the other hand neither of the combatants sounds particularly mature, so maybe June should use those lunch-hours studying so she can earn promotion for herself, either in this bank or some other field.

Lake is the second of the top trigrams and here we have the Mountain reversed, with the Earth (broken line) at the top and the peaks, the two sky lines making an indentation in the Earth forming the hollow of the lake.

One of the traditional virtues of the Lake is cheerfulness, and I have an image of a manic little Chinese lady whistling as she carries 17 buckets of water back from the lake. But the joy of the Lake comes from within, from pushing inside ourselves and finding the stillness, the balance and harmony that comes from there. This really is the trigram of withdrawal.

The wind and storms may ripple the surface of the lake and even make waves, but in the depths of both the Lake and the woman is the unchanging part, the real person that doesn't need dozens of friends or an exercise routine to define her self-worth. If you get this trigram, it's time to take the phone off the hook, tape up the doorbell and do anything, or absolutely nothing, but enjoy your own company. There are lots of times when we are forced to be alone and we can waste all that lovely time and energy when we are free from the demands of others, feeling abandoned and rejected. Lake says: 'OK, it's Friday night and you're not where the action is. So, no problems with late-night transport, stay at home, just you and your very best friend — yourself.'

A double Lake in the hexagram and there's probably been a sense that you are going

Day

10

The Lake trigram

Lake

through the motions of a busy, fulfilled life but have lost touch with yourself.

The danger in the Lake is of going so deep within yourself that you don't notice the chip pan is on fire, or the kids are bathing the dog with your best body oils.

Berenice's story

Berenice is in her early 60s and is the perfect granny and pivot of the small village in which she lives. She also acts as hostess, when helping out with her husband's charity work. And it's not a question of an ungrateful response, for she is loved and valued. But recently Berenice has felt she is acting on remote control and has increasingly found herself day-dreaming, forgetting appointments and even being grateful if an illness has kept her at home. Now she's been asked to become Regional Organiser for the local Women's Institute. But she is strangely reluctant to accept. Berenice draws two *yangs* and a *yin* on top.

The Lake trigram is urging her to step back for a while and follow her instinct to daydream and spend some time rediscovering herself, and her own needs and desires.

When we have a fulfilling life with lots of activity and people, it's easy to lose touch with ourselves. And then, when our mind starts withdrawing and forgetting appointments, we get worried instead of admitting that deep down we really want to miss those appointments, perhaps just for a while and let the world go by. It's not for ever, but there are times when we do need to recharge our batteries and withdraw, even from those we love, before we do get ill or depressed.

As I said, it's not forever and the beauty of the *I Ching* is that it does home in on the changes that are coming into our lives. So in the next chapter we'll go on to look at changing lines. But you may want to go back and spend a few days using the basic eight trigrams for readings and getting those definitions just right for you and your life. There are no fixed aspects of the *Ching* and all the ancients were doing (and all that I am trying to do) is to set down on paper what is essentially a practical system. So use the stones to get in touch with your inner well of insight and experience.

When better to start your own readings than now? You have seen how the trigrams work and how they have affected other people. But remember that your reading will be different from those you have encountered, because you are a different and unique person.

Your own readings

Don't worry if you do not recognise your trigram immediately. Consult the summary at the back of this book or re-read the relevant chapter.

Get your stones, then think of a general area of concern or a specific question. When you feel ready, draw a stone out of the bag without looking at it and place it on the table.

Which surface is uppermost? A *yin* or a *yang*? Now do the same with a second and third stone until they are in a vertical row of three.

Some people like to keep a *Ching* diary — nothing special, even a notebook will do — to record their trigram and what is happening in their life at the time. If you do this you can look back in weeks to come and see the changes in your life.

How often should you do a reading? Once you're on to hexagrams and change lines you may find a couple of times a week is enough. However, I use a daily trigram reading first thing in the morning just to set the mood of the day and see what's the most profitable way to react. All night you've been preparing, dreaming, waking with random thoughts, rehearsing or reliving those arguments, and a *Ching* reading in the morning is a good way of sifting through the best of your nocturnal meditations.

If I get the Earth trigram, for example, I wouldn't be planning on confronting an awkward colleague or handing in my notice. I might be planning the confrontation and even scanning the job columns, but this would be the time to do the spade work and absorb all I could get that might be useful when I do need to take some action. I know this on an unconscious level anyway, and the *Ching* will bring it to the surface.

You have your set of six basic *Ching* stones and, if you wish, you need to learn no more to give yourself (and others) perfectly good trigram readings that will answer any question you may ask (whether consciously or unconsciously). Be aware that sometimes what we think we are asking and what we really want to know are very different, but the *I Ching* is remarkably good at steering us in the right direction.

So if you don't immediately understand how your trigram applies, look at the issue in a broader context. Even if you do go on to the next two sections and learn the change lines and the hexagrams, trigram readings are very useful if you are in a hurry or have done a fuller reading recently. As I've said, some people (myself included) do a trigram every day to determine the approach most suitable to the day ahead.

As I have stressed, the *I Ching* is known as *The Book of Changes* which is why it is so useful in a world that is constantly changing. Our lives are rarely static for long periods. Even if the daily events sometimes seem toothachingly dull, life is more like a see-saw than a straight line. One minute you're on the up — the bathroom scales are reading half a stone lighter overnight, the sun is shining, you've been promoted and Mr Smooth is plying you with champagne and sending roses to your door (well, I can dream).

The next day the same see-saw goes down with a bump. You receive a letter from the bank saying your mortgage cheque has bounced, you've got PMT and Mr Smooth has turned into Master Octopus with moths in his purse.

And as a situation can change from moment to moment, so the Chinese believe that trigrams can change as well. This brings us to the change lines. You can read the *I Ching* without change lines but to use them enables you to follow your basic trigram through to what's waiting on the horzion. We will make a new set of stones with change lines — I'll explain how to do this further down — and when you pick stones using this new set, change lines may turn up in your basic trigram. On the other hand they may not, in which case you'll have to paddle like mad if you want to get your boat moving. If you turn over any change stones, you'll end up with a second trigram to mark out the route.

But first things first: the explanation. Certain *yang* lines were considered as *old yangs,* which were on the point of turning into *yin* lines. Remember that I said that *yangs* and *yins* were just two sides of the same coin.

These changing *yang* lines were written as —0—, rather like the London Underground sign, and quite different from the normal unbroken *yang* straight line, but we will use —0—for ease of writing.

Other lines were seen as *old yins* which would change into *yang* lines. These changing *yin* lines were written —✕—, whereas the normal *yin* was a broken line. Sounds complicated, but in fact it's very simple, so let's look at an example.

Fire

Using the old system you might get the trigram Fire:

But let's suppose we were using the changing stones. Now the top *yang* is a changing or *old yang* —0— and the middle *yin* is a change or *old yin* line —✕—. So the trigram would look like this, though it is still the trigram of Fire.

Since it is still Fire it has the usual meaning of clearing the way for reconstruction and renewal, putting your energy into practice, and has a message for your life as it is now. And you read it in exactly the same way as we did with the first Fire.

Day 13

The change lines (2)

Since this is more complicated I've taken an extra day. Fire is still fire as I said yesterday, but the change lines give us a bit of extra information. This additional message is that things are changing in your life just as the *old yin* —×— is changing to *yang* ——— and the *old yang* —0— is changing to *yin* ——. *So when we turn over the stones marked with change lines this gives us a second trigram of* Lake:

Lake

Lake represents the happiness that lies in looking to our inner resources, and taking a rest from all our activities, however enjoyable. So the *I Ching* may be telling you that although you are going through a period of Fire when you need to thrust yourself forward and communicate your ideas and experience to the rest of the world, you will need to follow this with a time of rest and relaxation (Lake) before you burn yourself out.

That, of course, is one reading of the changing trigram, but should it turn up for you, you must interpret it according to your own unique circumstances. For instance, it may be telling you that although your body is screaming for peace (Lake), a burst of activity (Fire) is needed before you can achieve it.

So how do we produce the change lines? As you would expect there are complicated traditional methods for deciding which are the change lines, but, as usual, we have an easier, quicker one.

First of all you will need to make a new set of *I Ching* stones. This time we need 12 to give us a full set for interpreting trigrams and hexagrams. Even if you decide to stick with trigrams for now you may want to move on later, so why not get the equipment ready?

So it's back to the beach or park and then find another bag or purse in which to keep Set Two of *I Ching* stones. You may wonder why I didn't suggest at the beginning of the book that you made these at the same time as the first set. Well, many of you may not want to make the changing *I Ching* stones. For, as I've said, you can use the plain stones to give trigram readings which are perfectly accurate, and if you do one every day or so, it will reflect the changes.

But it might be useful to read the rest of the book anyway so that when some know-all comes along and says, 'Aha, I see you're not using the change lines,' you can reply, 'Having studied them at great depth I find them irrelevant to my personal path'. Which is a polite way of telling him to get lost.

Even if you do make the second set of stones, you might still use your set of six plain *Ching* stones for a quick trigram reading, so it's best not to mix the two sets. I've got two different coloured sets as my kids tend to muddle my magic things up — nothing exotic, one set's brown and the other's grey. I tell the esoteric brigade those colours are closer to the earth! But in fact they're the colours found locally and picked up in record time — with five children, asking each pebble if it wants to be mine is a non-starter.

Why do we need 12 stones? This is because using the 24 faces will give us the four sets of six *yangs* and *yins* and their change lines for representative readings.

Don't forget your daily trigram reading. You might like to take your first set of stones with you and do a reading among the elements — powerful stuff even if you are sitting in a shelter in a wind-swept park. It makes the inner and outer worlds closer, which they should be. This is difficult if you work in a high-rise building where the greenery comes in pots and has flowers of perpetual plastic.

Day

15

When you have gathered your stones, disused draughts or counters, you will need your pen again.

On stone 1, draw a *yang* (——) unbroken line on one side of the pebble and then draw a change *yin* (—✕—) on the other side. Make five more pebbles marked like this.

On stone 7, draw a normal *yin* or broken line (— —) on one side of the pebble and on its other side draw the unbroken line with a circle in the middle (—0—).

Making the change stones (2)

Make five more pebbles marked like stone 7 and you then have your new set of change stones.

You will be making your trigrams in the usual fashion — it's just that now you have a wider range to choose from. Simply put the stones in the bag and draw out three at random, laying them one above the other as before.

Don't worry for now about the meaning, but keep making sets of three. Spend a bit of time recognising the different trigrams, using the new signs so the eight basic trigrams become second nature, however written. Don't forget you can use the first set of plain stones for your personal readings until you are sure of the new ones.

Day

16

Trigrams with change lines (1)

Now try a trigram with change lines. It's useful to look at the trigram before reading it and asking yourself how many change lines you have got. This tells you how stable the current situation is.

First read your trigram as usual, ignoring whether the *yin* and *yang* lines are changing or not.

Now turn over each of the changing lines in the trigram. (Leave the plain *yins* and *yangs* in place in the original trigram) and you'll see you've got a new trigram which tells you what's brewing. If you haven't got any change lines in the original trigram then things are staying as they are for now, so the stones won't make a second trigram today.

To look at the system in detail, let's study the reading I gave to Penny.

Penny's story

Penny is in her late teens and has left school against her parents' wishes, without taking her exams, to get a job in the local supermarket. Not surprisingly, Penny gets the Lake, the trigram of opting out of the fast lane in pursuit of her personal happiness. And of course if that is what she wants, then it is right for her. But it's a changing trigram, two ordinary *yangs* at the bottom and an *old yin* (—✕—) on top.

One change line out of three, so the change in her life won't be immediate.

This will give us a second trigram when we turn the change line over into three *yangs:* the Sky trigram.

Trigram 1: Lake.

The current situation will not last (the change line is at the top), but Penny may enjoy weeks or even months at her job before she gets the surge of energy that will catapult her to . . . where? The *Ching* won't reveal that because Penny hasn't yet made the decision. The *Ching* doesn't predict a fixed fate; what it does show is that forces are at work deep inside us that will make one way of responding to a situation the one most likely to bring happiness. In fact, the seeds are stirring right now in Penny, and she may decide to take advantage of the supermarket training scheme, or go to college in the evenings, or even expand her horizons in a more personal way.

Trigram 2: Sky.

It was only the scholars who defined the superior person as a civil servant. The *Ching* itself is about sky and water and growing trees so we shouldn't ever, in the *Ching* or life, be confined by other peoples' definitions of success.

Try a *Ching* trigram for yourself, using the change stones every morning. Remember, see if there is more than one change line, then read the trigram as normal, then turn over just the change lines (not the others). You now have a second trigram (without change lines) that shows the direction in which you may be moving.

Day 17

Trigrams with change lines (2)

Before moving on to hexagrams we'll do a second changing trigram that someone else drew, so that the idea becomes clearer. If you still aren't quite clear, read the section again — remember this is not a race and there are no prizes for dashing through the course in record time. The only prize is that, after learning the system to your own satisfaction, you can reap the benefits of it. You may decide that change lines are not for you, in which case you can stick with the trigrams or move on to hexagrams without change lines. *You* are in charge not me or anyone else.

The best way to learn is not by reading, but by turning over the stones time and time again until you carry the principle of the *I Ching* in your heart and mind.

Now let's see what the stones said to Emma.

Emma's story

Emma is a nurse in her mid-40s working nights in an old peoples' home, who finds her work load has increased to such an extent that she barely has time to stop for a 20-minute break. Her duties comprise, not only nursing and changing the beds of the very ill and incontinent old people she cares for, but also helping the care assistant prepare the breakfast for the next morning and sorting the dirty laundry ready for delivery.

Emma is aware that the owner is exploiting her, but knows that if she leaves her job the old people will miss her and perhaps not be so well cared for.

Emma draws the Earth trigram but with a change line at the bottom.

Trigram 1: Earth

So again, with only one change line, Emma won't be walking out tomorrow or even next week (some people get two or three change lines in a trigram — there are examples we'll meet later in the book, when the change idea is more familiar). The Earth trigram shows us what a caring person Emma is and the deep satisfaction she gets from that aspect of her job. It is this caring side that has held her back from demanding her rights. But sometimes pure Earth can lead to allowing exploitation to build up so that we can only stop it in the end by a life or death decision.

Change is on the way, however. And when the change line is turned over Emma has the Thunder trigram.

Trigram 2: Thunder

So Emma is going to find that the point is coming when she will need to demand adequate help with the routine tasks that take up valuable nursing time, if she is not to get to the point where she will say something she regrets. It's important for Emma to be aware of this so she can speak firmly and with authority before her patience does snap. And the danger in ignoring the impending Thunder forming within herself is that, if she does storm out, it gives the owner the opportunity to dismiss Emma's explosion as 'hysteria'. The real problem won't be solved, and that's not good either for Emma or the old people who depend on her.

Of course the *Ching* promises no automatic happy ending (it is about real life and not about fairy tales, oriental or otherwise). Emma may not get extra help even if she does ask calmly, but at least then she's got the chance to make a reasoned choice: either to leave, or put up with the situation, and cut corners in areas least likely to endanger the well-being of her charges.

If you are ready you can move on to the hexagrams — the sets of six lines. I would suggest you use the change lines only for trigram readings at the moment, and we will tackle the changing hexagrams later.

Day

18

Hexagrams

This section concentrates on the hexagrams, which are simply two trigrams one on top of the other to give six lines. So, while concentrating on the area of concern in your life, you would take six stones from the bag at random, placing the first at the bottom, the second above it, and so on. In the end you might have something like this:

Confusing? Not really, because if you look at it not as six lines, but two sets of three, you will see it turns into two trigrams.

Lake   *Tree*

This is called the Tree-Lake hexagram. It's not Lake-Tree because, remember, we read in the Chinese fashion from the bottom up.

Let's try another:

So this hexagram is:

Earth

Sky

Sky-Earth not Earth-Sky.

Spend some time today simply making hexagrams with your plain stones, and naming them using the bottom name followed by the top one. Once this is automatic you can then look at what they mean.

*Reading the
hexagram
(1)*

When it comes to reading the hexagram you need to consider how the two elements relate, and this time you picture them in the normal way regardless of the name: e.g. Lake is above the Tree.

Look back at yesterday's Tree-Lake hexagram and make it with your plain stones.

So here we have the Tree actually underneath the lake which immediately gives us a vision of floods and being, or simply feeling, submerged by things and finding it hard to keep afloat. It's like the times when the taxman casts his curse, and your least favourite relatives arrive with their suitcases for a surprise holiday just when you've stripped all the walls in the house to redecorate, or have got a deadline at work that involves working every evening for a month.

Most of the people I've met who make this hexagram say that drowning is exactly how they are feeling.

All very well but what can be done? What can the Tree do and, more importantly, what can we do in such a situation? Wait for the flood to go down: just do the essentials and let the rest go hang. Better still, offload the decorating onto the unwanted visitors — they'll soon remember an urgent date at the other end of the country.

But for now, the persistent, slow, gentle progress of the Tree (and you) is bogged down by one too many demands which means that accepting the situation where you try to do everything will only get you soggy wellies. For now, you need to cut those corners and give yourself as much rest and inner solitude as is possible until the present situation subsides.

Let's look at what this reading meant to someone else.

Maxine's story

Maxine is union treasurer at work and tends to be the unofficial counsellor for the women members who come to her with their problems. Now she has been asked to take on the position of women's rep for the county, which will mean she will tackle problems on an official level rather than the present informal basis. Her fellow workmates see this as a chance for her to take on the management on their behalf over a range of grievances, but her own career prospects depend on her treading a delicate path with her male bosses, who see the new position as an act of treachery. The area organisers are also eager for Maxine to set a precedent for certain issues by challenging her own management. Maxine feels that she is being used as a pawn for other people, and feels totally overwhelmed and wishes she'd never got involved.

Her Tree-Lake hexagram confirms that she is being overwhelmed by conflicting demands, not least her own need to keep on good terms with her bosses. She has reached the stage where she can't sleep for worrying and is getting dreadful headaches. So the only thing she can do is to wait, and not take on the new formal post. She can use her own ill-health as a reason and before long a new Boudicca will emerge to take her place, or the chaps at Area Office will find a new cause to support. Maxine can then go on with her excellent informal approach to women's issues at work.

But if you get the Tree-Lake hexagram it might have an entirely different meaning for you.

The hexagrams give us a lot to think about, so for the moment I suggest you stick to trigram readings while we consider hexagrams in detail over the next few days.

Reading the hexagram (2)

Before we start hexagram readings, let's recap on what we learned over the past two days. It's worth spending a bit of time on the basics so that they become automatic. Otherwise it's like driving a car when you're looking for the brake and don't see the double-decker bus parked ahead.

Remember a hexagram is just two trigrams stacked up and we read from the bottom up.

As an exercise, try identifying these hexagrams. Don't worry if you have to look up the trigrams to refresh your memory. This is not an exam. You are learning a system in your own time, on your own terms, to help yourself. Don't worry about the meanings just yet. Because the meanings will change as your life changes.

The hexagrams are:

You may like to try this exercise with your stones, picking them at random and then identifying the hexagrams — not to ask questions but just to ensure that the system becomes second nature to you. Because, when you have a real crisis in your life, you want to be able to fire off the questions and work out the answers without having to consult a book every other moment.

The hexagrams that you have just looked at were: 1 Fire-Sky, 2 Water-Tree, and 3 Lake-Earth. Don't worry if you didn't get them right first time — you will with practice.

Let's look at someone else's hexagram.

A sample hexagram reading

Hilary's story

Hilary is in her late 20s and feels frustrated because she is tied at home with three young children. She regrets not finishing her university degree and leaving college to get married when she became pregnant. She is bored with coffee mornings and helping at playgroup and wants to do something for herself. She has toyed with the idea of taking an Open University course, but is put off because, even with her exemptions, it will take six years to complete an honours degree.

Using the *I Ching* stones, Hilary draws first a *yin* (broken line), then two *yangs* (unbroken lines). That gives her the first trigram of the Tree.

Many people do find it helpful to read the trigram first before forming the second part of the hexagram to sit on top of it. So straight away we've got gentle perseverance, inch by inch.

Tree

Now let's look at the trigram that will sit above Tree. Hilary draws three *yins* (broken lines) and that gives us the Earth trigram.

Earth

And, of course, we have good old Mother Earth Hilary, caring and nurturing and feeling a bit as if she's lost her own identity. Remember the *I Ching* image of Earth as an old cart to dump everything in. Another ancient idea is Earth (the receptive one) as a seamless cloak (not a lot of personal outline). And that's what Hilary is feeling.

Now put the trigrams together, remembering the bottoms-up rule, ie, that the first trigram (Tree) we drew will go first, at the bottom.

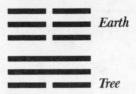

Earth

Tree

And that's all a hexagram is. Now look at the image of the trigrams put together. Make it with your stones. So we've got a picture of a Tree below the Earth. So Hilary is still very rooted in her home situation, and her potential is well and truly hidden in the caring role. But that would make the Open University a viable option, starting to prepare for a new career from where she is right now.

A tree begins to make its impact on the world as a small shoot pushing its way slowly and with perseverance through the earth. Hilary should perhaps accept that her path will be a slow one and that six years isn't an eternity. Once the children are at school she will be able to increase the number of courses she takes each year. Hilary added all sorts of ideas of her own, about how the tree had to withstand the frosts and difficulties of the first stages, but how it would get easier and, even if things only happened slowly, she would be moving upwards out of her domestic rut. In fact once I'd explained the basic meaning of the trigrams (though she'd never encountered the *Ching* before) she didn't need me at all.

Now let's look at something we have already touched on: the doubling principle — when you get the same trigrams stacked up.

Double Sky: The Energy Hexagram

▬▬▬▬ *Sky*

▬▬▬▬ *Sky*

Our old friend has masses and masses of energy and new ideas that are carefully formulated and thought through. So something new is afoot — and it's not a new knitting pattern. The spark is inside but it's also in your everyday world. Put the two together and Wow!

Let's see what Double Sky said to Paula.

Paula's story

Paula found herself separated from her partner of 20 years, who had sapped her confidence before running off with a younger model when his mid-life hormones started churning. The question was not, 'What next?' but 'Dare I?' Paula was left with a few thousand pounds and a long-standing dream. She had costed and planned many, many times starting a design business, based on reasonable prices and individual styles, for women whose hip sizes reflected that they were flesh and blood not broom handles. Since half the population are size 16 and over, she was obviously onto a winner in a small town where the boutiques catered only for the size 12s and under.

The Double Sky showed Paula that the lingering doubts she had resulted from years of being undermined, but they were yesterday's message. And she went for it!

So remember, the double appearance of a trigram makes its meaning doubly strong. However, you must still work out for yourself what the trigram is saying to you personally, at that particular moment in your life. Sticking to a rigid definition instead of listening to your inner voice could mean you get it doubly wrong!

Day

23

An example of the doubling principle

As doubling is an important principle, let's look at just one more example before we go on. Remember that these examples are here only to help you and are not set in stone. You will probably find as you progress with the *I Ching* that you don't want to give a specific all-time name, all-place definition to your hexagrams, but prefer to work them out as you go by looking at the picture the two elements create — and this may well differ from situation to situation. And there's no right or wrong definition because everyone combines the elements according to their own unconscious needs and intuitions.

Or you may decide that you want to buy a giant volume of the full *I Ching* and study its words in depth. You can still use your *I Ching* stones to produce the trigrams and hexagrams (I find that yarrow stalks are usually out of stock at my corner grocery shop) and you will still need to call on your inner voice to interpret the oracle. The important thing is that you use a system that suits you.

Personally, I tend to use a floating definition according to the situation and the person. I find it amazing that the ancients should have tried to tie down what is *The Book of Changes* with so many restrictions. But then, if it had got around that anybody could do it, Mr Confucius and the Emperor Wen might have ended up having to stir their own dish of tea.

First of all see if you can recognise this hexagram:

It is, of course, Double-Earth. As I have said, Earth is the intuition trigram and this is a double dose. The power expressed here comes from that knowledge you absorb naturally, as you go about fulfilling the 1001 other demands on your time. It draws on the wisdom of your deep unconscious which, if it is allowed to gain expression, gives you the right answer first time. So if you instinctively distrust someone, even though he has a city suit and a CV longer than your supermarket bill, then you are most likely right not to give him control over your finances, or your heart. Trust your instincts. This is what happened to Madge who drew the Double-Earth.

Madge's story

Madge is in her late 20s and on the verge of selling her flat and giving up her job. She will then be moving abroad to live with her new boyfriend, a Spaniard, whose family own the holiday complex where she spent her holiday. She and Carlos are going to buy a large apartment overlooking the sea and she will help administer the holiday complex. So why should Madge hesitate? Carlos is charming, the family are welcoming and she has no ties in England.

Madge makes the Double Earth hexagram and so, it seems, all her lovely caring qualities are going to find fulfilment through her new relationships: both the guests whom she will help have a good holiday and all those lovely children she and Carlos will be having. But what is her intuition trying to tell her?

Madge voiced a few 'what ifs' when she made the hexagram. She felt that she was being carried along to a permanent arrangement before she was ready. Carlos was very considerate to her, but she'd seen a very chauvinistic side to his older male relatives in their own homes, and felt that Carlos was influenced very strongly by his older brothers and father. So? After a lot of pressure, which she resisted, Madge decided to go over to Spain for six months, rent out her flat in England and keep in touch with vacancies in her career back home — just in case.

Of course, in different circumstances the inner voice might tell you to trust your Carlos when everyone else is decrying him as a rotter. Remember, your destiny is your own.

The other very important principle to remember with hexagrams is stacking. As you
know by now, we read from bottom up so
that:

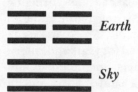 *Earth*

Stacking

Sky

is Sky-Earth not Earth-Sky. Would it make any
difference if you got it round the other way?
Yes, in fact it might be vital. Let's look at two
contrasting readings.

In the Sky-Earth hexagram, pure *yang* has
pure *yin* above it. The positive and negative
charges are making contact and *yang* and *yin*
combine to make a complete whole.

Its traditional name is peace, in the sense of
harmony, and the idea of the balanced
approach is a useful one, just the right
amount of logic and intuition, caring and self-
preservation, speaking and listening. Hang
on, you say, Sky should be above the Earth!
But if it was, as we see in the later Earth-Sky
trigram, old Sky is letting all that energy float
away, and as for Earth, well she's tunnelling
down to her mole hole. It would be like putting the batteries in your torch the wrong
way round.

You're very much on the right track if you
make this hexagram. And your inner ideas
and ambitions are being applied in very

practical, down to earth ways that don't steam roller over anyone, but do transform the mundane. Take 10 Brownie points.

Angie's story

Angie made Sky-Earth when she started to take a teaching course after ten years at home bringing up the children. Though life was hard, fitting in home and study commitments, Angie had more life and energy than she'd had for years and, after a few initial hiccups, she'd persuaded the kids and her husband either to lend a hand or not complain if things weren't up to scratch. But then mother-in-law arrived for an annual visit and threw up her hands in horror at the state of the house, and set about giving it a good spring clean. She told Angie that the children and her husband were being neglected on a whim and, since there was no need financially for Angie to work, she was being selfish.

Angie drew the Sky-Earth, 'right on course' hexagram which gave her the confidence to tell ma-in-law, ever so nicely, that the shop down the road was doing a nice line in broomsticks so maybe she'd like to fly home.

Sky

Earth

By contrast Earth-Sky is the 'wasted effort' hexagram, for here the batteries are the wrong way round and are not producing any charge. You are burrowing away deeper and deeper in the earth and getting tired and frustrated, giving of your best, seemingly for nothing — the ideas or relationships concerned are no nearer fruition than on Day 1. So give up.

Mary's story

Mary is a healer in her 60s and has been struggling to keep a group going while the other members are locked in grandiose plans for their own personal development. She is feeling tired and dispirited, and so much of her energy is dissipated trying to keep peace between the other members and to meet the needs of the patients, that she fears she is losing her own gift.

Her Earth-Sky hexagram suggests that her own efforts to care for her fellow healers aren't having any real effect and indeed are draining her of the energy for her own healing work. Eventually Mary decides to close the group for a while and carry on with her healing alone.

You should by now have a pretty good understanding of the hexagrams and the basic principles of doubling and combining the elements. So try you own readings, taking six stones from your *I Ching* bag at random and building the hexagram from the bottom. If you find it easier, pause at your first three stones and see what the first trigram is saying to you before continuing with the second. Then combine the elements and consider what they mean in your life.

I will give you one more example before we move on, but remember — this is what the *I Ching* was saying to one particular person at a particular stage of her life.

Heather's story

Heather is in her early 50s and a teacher of handicapped children. She has been asked by her Head Teacher to go on a course to obtain a higher diploma that will enable her to train other members

Day

25

Reading your own hexagram

of staff. But Heather's elderly mother-in-law has recently moved in with her and seems to be showing early signs of dementia. Though Heather is caring for her mother-in-law as well as working full-time, her husband Paul is complaining that she no longer supports him in his work as a Rotary Member.

Heather draws Lake as her first trigram:

Lake

This shows her retreating into herself. She said that this was apt, as she had been aware recently of just going through the motions of her life and almost welcomed her migraines as a chance to opt out. She was dreading the thought of adding studies to her busy life and dreamed of doing nothing.

Her second trigram is Water:

Water

Again, this trigram is about going with the flow rather than making a decision. So does it mean she should go on the course that is offered? This is where the hexagram scores over the trigram — remember our Water example in the second chapter, and the unemployed lady who was being pushed to follow a retraining programme though she could see no purpose. But here the Water is above the lake and so we have the water from the sky (rain) pouring into the lake.

Water

Lake

Now Heather's lake is getting pretty full and if people keep raining demands on her, she won't be able to cope. A lake can hold only so much water and Heather can only do so much. So she's got to limit herself to what she can manage without being deluged, and give herself that vital time she needs to do nothing and to be herself. So for now, the course might not be a good idea and since charity begins at home, Paul must be made to play his part in caring for his mother, even if this cuts down on his outside good works.

Now you know the *I Ching* hexagrams, you are ready to unleash yourselves on the waiting world. I've been saying this since you learned the eight basic trigrams, because the beauty of this system is that you can learn as much or as little as you wish and still get readings that are relevant to your life. Some women swear by using the trigrams, plain and simple, as a mood indicator, and, if used regularly, they can show what is just out of your eye-shot, though not out of range of your in-built radar.

Then there is the trigram plus change lines, a bit more fine-tuning that is especially good for seeing round corners. After that came the hexagrams, built up by combining the two trigram meanings, which are remarkably accurate and very sensitive. The last few chapters have given you my interpretations of a few of the 64 hexagrams, based on the old ideas.

At the back is a summary of what we've learned, but before that is an extra section of my own ideas of what the 64 hexagrams mean to me. But, as I have said, these definitions are not meant to be learned by heart, just referred to if you get stuck on a particular hexagram or trigram, but I have allowed some of our 42 days for you to read them, maybe make those you are interested in and hopefully develop your own ideas. You might like to have a quick skim through now.

This final section looks at the changing hexagram, so it's out with those dozen change stones we made earlier. Again you don't have to do more than skim this chapter if you decide that you want to keep the hexagrams plain and simple. I tend to use whichever type of reading is most useful at the time and the changing hexagram does give a high degree of fine-tuning when you are trying to sense what is in the air, or bubbling beneath the surface.

Use the change stones as we did for the changing trigrams, only this time we will have six lines that may all change. It sounds like a lot but remember, all the hexagram is is two trigrams, one on top of the other. Don't worry about rising and falling lines that you may hear about or strong and weak lines in more complicated books on the subject. Should you become an *I Ching* Mistress, then you can easily gen up on them later. Under my system just remember three points.

First: Count the number of change lines you have got. The more there are, the closer the change is. If you've got six then you've barely time to grab your hat.

Second: Look at the hexagram, does the shape suggest anything? Some people are remarkably good at seeing pictures in shapes, but I'm one of the people who can't put a three-piece jigsaw together if the pieces are upside down. If you can, then you may see gateways, open mouths biting through obstacles, or the like, and this can help you to work out your destiny.

Third: Turn over the changing stones to produce your second hexagram and see what this suggests to you. But remember there are no rights or wrongs — how can there be when we are dealing with a changing world where the unconscious pressures and influences may be far stronger than the conscious?

Don't forget your own hexagram and trigram readings — you should be building up a tale to rival any Chinese masterpiece of the ups and downs and straights — my *Ching* diary looks like a sea-sick snake.

Day 28

So let's take a changing hexagram, a mobile one with six change lines and look at the life of the woman who drew it. Then you can try one.

Fire   *Water*

The changing hexagram — an example

Here we've got the 'damp squib' hexagram, when people or circumstances well and truly put a damper on your brave new steps to put your ideas into action.

Kate's story

That is just what happened to Kate when she enrolled for her first year of Open University. Her husband and teenage kids did everything possible to discourage her — often families feel threatened when good old Mum tries to spread her wings — and she was two essays behind and all ready to throw in the towel.

So what's the point in a hexagram telling you what you already know? Well, for a start, those six change lines indicate that there's a crisis point looming up pretty fast, and either Kate will give up for good and go back to being dear old Mum, or she'll start swimming like mad and say, 'Blow you lot, get your own tea till I've caught up on those essays. And if I want to go to summer school for a week, then I will.'

So what will she do? Let's watch her turn over the stones. The new hexagram won't give her the cast iron answer, but it will remind her of what she really wants and feels deep down. Of course, we don't always do what we know we should, but if Kate really wants to turn that damp squib into a firework, she has the inner resources.

For what we've now got is Fire-Water, a very different kettle of fish.

This is the 'Keeping up the momentum' hexagram, with the water singing in the kettle. But it's not the easy option. It reminds Kate of her high hopes when she began the course, and all those plans for organising her family life so she could succeed. And now it's time to implement those plans and keep the momentum going. She's got to stoke that fire of achievement and it's going to take a hard slog.

Now try a change hexagram of your own, using the twelve change stones — remember that you only take six of them. Simply lay out the two trigrams one on top of the other and read as usual, ignoring the changes. So —0— you'll read as a normal *yang* and —×— as a normal *yin*. When you've worked out what the hexagram is saying, count the change lines to see how imminent or urgent the change is.

Then turn over the change lines to make your new hexagram. Don't turn over the ordinary *yangs* or *yins*. Read the second hexagram, (at first, as two trigrams if that helps) and see how the two hexagrams fit together in your life. You might like to note them down in your *Ching* diary, together with a brief line about what is happening around you. Then you can see what patterns are emerging as you take conscious control of your life, using all those hidden powers of intuition and inspiration that are at your disposal. But, of course, you don't have to write anything down because you can make the hexagrams in the stones, though I find my *Ching* diary very useful in reminding me of my resolutions.

Another example of a changing hexagram

While you are getting the hang of the hexagram with change lines let's look at another example.

Sally's story

Sally's Mountain-Earth had four change lines which suggests that the change wasn't too far off, though not immediate.

Earth

Mountain

This is the hexagram of hidden ambitions and, though it often appears when a woman is submerged in the care of others, it hints that she holds dreams of doing her own thing that perhaps could begin in a small way now. Sally works as a teacher and is also a wife, mother and grandmother. Her dream is to go back alone for a month, almost as a pilgrimage, to the Italian village where she lived as a child, and where she spent so many happy hours. She wants to try to recapture some of its beauty on camera. Her husband is happy, so long as he can go along, and says if she loved him she wouldn't want to go off. Her children and grandchildren think Mum is just sulking and wouldn't last five minutes on her own. She has been saving for her trip for quite a while and will have a month's sabbatical due in six months' time. But the kids say she should spend the money on a family holiday.

The hexagram changes to Water-Lake.

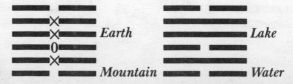

Earth

Mountain

Lake

Water

This may seem a strange answer because it's the hexagram of feeling drained, as though you haven't got any more to give. But what it's saying to Sally is, if you give up your dream for a family holiday, you will be losing part of yourself. For Sally has given so much over the years that this dream is almost a last ditch attempt to say 'I'm me, apart from you'.

So what can she do? Clearly she shouldn't fight and argue, which will drain her more. Of course, she can't hand over her savings to keep the peace and finance a holiday which the family could well afford to pay for. It's a time for conserving energy and making her own plans, perhaps agreeing that after her trip they will all take a family holiday, to which all contribute fairly.

Now try another reading for yourself, concentrating on the big issues of the moment in your life.

Day

30

Reflecting on the Ching

As you have discovered, it is very simple to make a change hexagram and it can be a good way of clarifying a difficult situation. We've only taken a month to get through the basics, which leaves 14 days to read through my hexagram definitions, try them out yourself and replace then with your own. I leave you with your two sets of stones and this book as a pointer. But the real wisdom of the *Ching* is your inner well of unconscious wisdom that you carry in your heart and soul. And your stones can help you to tap that inner magic that enables you to see the warning signs, the impending tidal wave that can carry you to new shores if you are prepared, but will swamp you if you leave life to chance. Life is full of changes, but if we can acknowledge them and use them in a positive way then we can be mistress and not slave of our destiny.

This takes us back to Mrs Confucius, with her quiet smile sweeping up the yarrow stalks, as the great men obscure the simple beauty behind the *Ching,* with their social codes that were no fairer to women 3,000 years ago than they are now.

As you are jammed in the train between Surbiton and Waterloo, look up at the sky and at the dingy stretches of water that were once mighty rivers. See the lake which the gravel pit might be, the trees crammed between the new housing estates, mountains that rise in your mind above the cluttered streets. See the fire in the storm and the lightning in the thunder and open your windows to welcome the power that man will never control or tame. Whether you live, as I do now, in a rural area, backed by downs and sea, or in a place like my childhood home in central Birmingham, where the earth fought for space between the paving stones, go out, if you can, to the top of a hill or a beach or even the local park and feel the power behind the stones that is part of you. And then go back to family, friends and work, and carve out the little bit of the world that belongs solely to you.

You do not need to memorise this section but you may find it useful to spend some days reading my definitions, seeing how women applied them to their situations and making the hexagrams for yourself. But your feelings about the images and what they mean to you may be different from mine. Feel free to change them. Remember this is a system to suit you, not anybody else.

The
Hexagrams
in daily life

I've allowed 12 days of our six-week course for this reading — but you may go through it faster or more slowly or prefer to wait until the hexagrams turn up in your own readings before consulting my definitions and seeing how they fit in with your experiences.

The hexagrams are arranged in blocks of eight but read them any way you wish — maybe you'll come up with a better way of organising them. You will recognise a few readings from the main book. I've included them here so you can see where they fit into the general pattern and with other hexagrams of the same type. I hope you'll write to me with your significant hexagrams especially if you have entirely different images from mine.

Remember if people tell you this isn't the real *I Ching*, that the *I Ching* was a visual and oral system thousands of years before it was written down. And just as a Chinese picture if analysed is just a series of lines — taken as a whole and interpreted according to your own inner world you can see rivers, lakes and mountains. Images, thrown from your mind, are the essence of the true *I Ching* and for many people the overlay of commentaries over the centuries have taken us further from the natural world that Taoists, and many Western systems such as Druidism, believe we are part of.

The forces of *Water, Fire, Earth* and *Sky* are within us all and though we may begin using *I Ching* to guide our everyday actions it can lead us to great insights into our own spirituality if we trust ourselves to relate with it and not merely read the judgements of others, however wise they may seem.

SKY

There are eight Sky hexagrams (six liners) where three yangs form the bottom trigram. If in doubt, think of the lower trigram in terms of your inner world and the upper one as reflecting the everyday outer sphere.

Double-Sky — the Energy hexagram. Masses and masses of energy and new ideas that are carefully formulated and thought through. Something new is afoot and it's not a new knitting pattern. The spark is inside but it's also in your everyday world.

Sky

Sky

When Paula was deserted by her partner of twenty years she was left with a few thousand pounds and a long-standing dream to start a design business for larger-sized women. Since half the population are Size 16 and over she was obviously on to a winner in a small town where the boutiques catered only with teenies and tinies.

Her Double-Sky showed Paula that any lingering doubts, developed over the years of being undermined, were yesterday's message and she went for it!

Sky-Earth — the 'Right on Course' hexagram. Whatever anyone else says, you're very much on the right track. Your inner ideas and ambitions are being applied in very practical ways that transform the mundane.

Earth

Sky

Angie started to take a teaching course after ten years at home bringing up the children. Though it was hard fitting in home and study commitments, Angie had more life and energy than she'd had for years. But then her mother-in-law arrived for an annual visit and threw her hands up in horror at the state of the house and told Angie that the children and her husband were being neglected.

Angie drew the Sky-Earth, 'right on course' hexagram which gave her the confidence to tell ma-in-law ever so nicely that the shop down the road was doing a nice line in broomsticks so maybe she'd like to fly home.

Sky-Fire — the 'Off the Top of your head' hexagram is about the sheet of lightning illuminating the sky which makes you forget about going from A to C via B by cutting out all the steps in between by using not intuition but inspiration.

Fire

Sky

Abbie was set for a three-year course at university after school but she really wanted to work abroad for a year and see the world. Her parents said this would be a backward step and she'd just drift. She drew the Sky-Fire hexagram and suddenly a third solution appeared — was it magic or was she, for the first time, considering a new approach? She applied and got an official exchange programme to the United States that would enable her to see the country but continue to study and was able to defer her university place for a year.

Sky-Water — the 'waiting for the right moment' hexagram says the idea is inside us and the energy to make that new start, but if we go before the starter's orders, before the rain clouds have given us the river to follow we'll only waste all that lovely power.

Water

Sky

Jean is in her late fifties. Her husband's womanising and heavy drinking have long since destroyed all feeling she had for her partner. In a year's time her youngest daughter will be starting college and an insurance policy will mature, giving her some capital of her own. Her recently widowed sister is urging her to move to Majorca with her as a permanent house guest, though they have never been close.

Jean draws the Sky-Water hexagram. And it confirms the feeling in her heart of hearts that to move in now with a sister she doesn't get on all that well with is a bit like jumping out the frying pan into the fire.

Sky-Thunder — the 'Heavy-Handed' hexagram, says that sometimes force isn't the best way with a new idea or regime. There may be plenty of power behind you but even if you're certain you are 200 per cent right, go gently.

Thunder

Sky

Joanne's teenage children are being particularly obnoxious, staying out half the night and refusing to lift a finger. Joanne has all the expense, noise and hassle while her ex-husband has a quiet civilised life and visits the children only once a month. Recently she discovered her elder child has been truanting from school and she has told the children that after the holidays they can live with their father, full stop.

Joanne draws the Sky-Thunder hexagram. Understandable though her reaction is, it may be that there is a more subtle approach that will ram her message home. How about a long·holiday with Dad who agonises over buying them so much as a can of Coke on access visits? Well, three or four weeks of the Terrible Teenies should make him take steps to ensure they behave better with mum. As for the adolescents, no home comforts and the loss of the maternal money box, should make them come back whistling and singing 'There's no place like home.'

Sky-Tree — the 'Subtle Approach' hexagram. We've got our old friend the Tree pushing skywards inch by inch. By starting with small changes you can whittle away at that seemingly immovable status quo.

Tree

Sky

Catriona has met the 'glass ceiling' in action. Although she is highly qualified in computers, she is being pushed more and more to cover for absences in the customer relations department of her firm because 'women are good at dealing with problems'. Now there's a permanent vacancy in that section and Catriona has been suggested for the job as the only woman in the department.

She draws the Sky-Tree hexagram and so it would seem that she's not going to change entrenched attitudes overnight. But there's no harm in suggesting that a rota system is adopted so that they all take a turn dealing with the public and that when it is Catriona's turn she does a good PR job of emphasising the caring qualities of her male colleagues to the boss of the Customer Section.

Sky-Mountain — the 'hidden Treasure Hexagram'. Sky's energy is hidden within the mountain. What we're really talking about is using your inner skills and talents in a practical way to further your everyday existence.

Mountain

Sky

Philippa was made redundant from the insurance company where she'd spent all her working life and at fifty there wasn't a lot of chance of getting another job. But Philippa was a keen gardener and a friend who had land round her house was thinking of starting a market garden. Should Philippa put her redundancy money into the business or try to invest it to supplement her income from the state?

Philippa drew the Sky-Mountain hexagram suggesting the inner energy and her knowledge of plants is at the moment static in the mountain which is the outer life that has for now come to a standstill. So the market garden would be a way of utilising talents that have so far been a hobby.

Sky-Lake — the hexagram of 'breaking through the barriers' because the lake has risen to the level of the sky and overcome those obstacles in a waterfall. The important thing is to use this sudden impetus to make the move we may have dreamed about and not worry about tomorrow.

Lake

Sky

Claire has always wanted to be a writer and at last has had an idea accepted and been given a small advance to write a book. Using her savings she can manage for a year or so but her friends are telling her she would be a fool to throw up a secure job for a future with no guarantees.

She draws the Sky-Lake hexagram. So her inner dreams - in this case of writing a book - have chance of becoming reality and if she doesn't go for it, she may always regret the lost chance.

EARTH

The Earth hexagrams are concerned with the intuitive, nurturing aspect of a woman's life.

Double-Earth — the hexagram of intuition, draws on the wisdom of your deep unconscious and if it is allowed to gain expression, gives you the right answer first time.

Earth

Earth

Madge is in her late twenties and on the verge of selling her flat and giving up her job and moving abroad to live with her new boyfriend, a Spaniard whose family own the holiday complex where she spent her holiday. So why should Madge hesitate? Carlos is charming, the family are welcoming and she has no ties in England.

Madge makes the Double-Earth hexagram and so it seems all her lovely caring qualities are going to find fulfilment through her new relationships. So what is her intuition trying to tell her? Madge felt that she was being carried along to a permanent arrangement before she was ready. After a lot of pressure which she resisted Madge decided to go over to Spain for six months and rent out rather than sell her flat in England just in case.

Earth-Sky, the 'wasted effort' hexagram in life and relationships. You are burrowing away deeper and deeper in the earth and getting tired and frustrated, giving of your best seemingly for nothing — the ideas or relationship is no nearer fruition than on day one. Cut your losses.

Sky

Earth

Mary is a healer in her sixties and has been struggling to keep a group going while other members are locked in grandiose plans for their own personal development. Mary is feeling tired and dispirited and so much of her energy is dissipated trying to keep peace between the other members and meet the needs of the patients, she fears she is losing her own gift.

She makes the Earth-Sky hexagam which suggests that her own efforts to care for her fellow healers aren't having any real effect and indeed are draining her of the energy for her own healing work. Eventually Mary decided to close the group for while and carry on with her healing alone.

Earth-Fire — the 'tomorrow is another day' hexagram. The sun will rise above the earth again, no matter how bad things seem right now. Don't dwell on today's disasters.

Fire

Earth

Trudy has daughter-in-law trouble. And last week she spoke her mind rather too forcefully.

Sarah hadn't been slow in responding with her grievances. So now there is total silence between the households and Trudy fears she won't ever see her grandchildren again. She can't sleep for worrying.

Trudy makes the Earth-Fire hexagram so perhaps it's time Trudy as the older – and hopefully wiser – combatant accepts that what's said can't be unsaid but should offer an olive branch and see if there can't be a new perhaps more realistic start based on sounder foundations.

Earth-Water — the hexagram of 'adapting to the situation'. When we are in a less than ideal situation, it may be better to modify our plans accordingly rather than giving up or waiting for the obstacle to clear.

Water

Earth

After six years' legal training May found herself unable to get a job in the field she had dreamed of from early childhood. All that was on offer was a post in industrial law which would involve extra on the job training and a path she wasn't sure she wanted to take. Her

Earth-Water hexagram suggested that it might be better to adapt her ideas and at least make some forward move in her career, rather than wait for a dream job which might not materialise.

Earth-Thunder — **the hexagram of 'bringing the situation to a head'** seen in the old imagery as the first electrical storm bursting from the earth in summer. Suddenly all those unresolved issues that have been lying dormant get a sudden and sometimes shocking boost to solve them one way or the other.

Thunder

Earth

Debbie is in her mid-forties and has been through a very difficult trial separation. Her parents have suggested she moves back home but she has resisted this, as one of the problems in her marriage has been her close involvement with her parents, which caused her husband to feel excluded. Just recently she and her husband have been meeting and really talking to each other for the first time in years. Out of the blue he has challenged her to move right away to Wales with him and open the cafe they always dreamed of if she is serious about their marriage.

The Earth-Thunder hexagram shows that her husband's challenge means that matters can't lay unresolved forever and now is the time to get up and go if she wants to save her marriage. Only Debbie can choose.

Earth-Tree — the 'considering the options' hexagram. Sometimes we need to stop and look at all the pros and cons of a situation for ourselves, especially where the decision has implications for others who depend on us, rather than asking for advice or just hoping for the best.

Tree

Earth

Gilda is unhappy in her job as a secretary, but the hours are flexible so she can take time off when one of her children are ill. Since she works for a building society she has a cheap mortgage which is essential as she is struggling alone to pay it. Her friends say it's not worth the hassle and a few times Gilda has nearly walked out because of her immediate boss's bad temper.

Gilda makes the Earth-Tree hexagram and we can see that her job is essential for providing for her family so pulling up roots won't be easy. For now the only answer seems to be to wait and contemplate the alternatives. Not a very encouraging hexagram though it does contain the option that she can look around for alternative employment.

Earth-Mountain the 'shaky foundations' hexagram, can be pictured as the earth crumbling away and eroding the mountain. When this hexagram appears it's as well to check the small print in any contract, whether financial or emotional.

Mountain

Earth

Josephine who is in her mid-fifties inherited money from her mother's estate and, her boyfriend Phil suggested she invest the money in a company he was forming based on producing computerised birthday greetings. The idea was clearly a good one but this was Phil's fourth commercial venture and the previous three had foundered under the realities of marketing and distribution problems.

Josephine's Earth-Mountain hexagram reflects her own fears that this is yet another of Phil's grandiose schemes. Loans are maybe best left to banks and if Josephine can steer Phil to this, then he will be forced to cost and work out the logistics. Maybe the mountain won't get built in the first place, or at least if it only turns out to be a hill, have a firm basis.

Earth-Lake — the hexagram of 'taking on too much'. The water is rising above the sides of the lake warning you that you're almost at the limit of what you can comfortably take on. So start saying no now before the pressures get too great.

Lake

Earth

Esther has been in this situation many times before. A foster mother and loving grandmother her philosophy is that there is always room for another child in her home and in her heart. But on previous occasions when she has taken on one too many placements she has found herself becoming increasingly short-tempered with her own family. Usually she has come down with an illness and then chaos has broken loose.

Recently Esther has been doing additional respite care for distressed families as well as her normal fostering. Now she has been asked to take over the running of the local toddler group which wants to develop a policy of encouraging handicapped children to come along unaccompanied to give the parents a break.

Esther makes the Earth-Lake hexagram which warns her that her tolerance is closer to breaking than she realises so she limits her new role to an advisory one.

FIRE

The eight Fire hexagrams talk about giving form to new ideas and communication.

Double-Fire — the hexagram of 'clear communication' says it is important to express precisely what you want. Equally it is essential to listen to what the other person is actually saying and not what you assume they may be implying.

Fire

Fire

Ruth is seventy and recently widowed. She felt totally unable to cope with life without her husband on whom she depended for all practical and financial matters. She told her married daughter that she was going to sell her house immediately and move in with her. Her daughter refused abruptly and both have ended up not speaking at a time when real communication is vital.

Ruth made the Double-Fire hexagram which suggests that her communication to her daughter, though apparently clear enough, was not expressing her real feelings and that her daughter's refusal was not, whatever it seemed, a sign she didn't care. What Ruth really wanted was reassurance that she wouldn't be abandoned and what her daughter was saying was that while she was prepared to offer her mother support, she didn't want her life permanently taken over.

Fire-Sky, the hexagram of 'fanning the flames', warns us that the fire can get out of control, if you aren't careful. A potentially explosive situation is not the place to start making ultimatums, but for trying to find a way to sidestep the immediate problem.

Sky

Fire

Stephanie's grandmother strongly objects to her boyfriend because he is Asian and refuses to invite him to her eighty-fifth birthday party. Stephanie says she won't go either and will tell everyone why. Her mother, who likes Imran very much, says the old lady is being unreasonable but, the party is the first major family get together for years and given granny's age and health may be the last. She suggests it might be better to arrange a family meeting to introduce Imran to the other relations the day after the party.

Stephanie makes the Fire-Sky hexagram and so she realises that her boycott wouldn't make gran any fonder of Imran but would cause a family crisis at a time which, like most family gatherings, will be tense enough. Maybe it is one of those occasions when Stephanie needs to accept the invitation without comment and then get a last minute headache or make her visit to the party a brief one.

Fire-Earth, the hexagram of 'hidden emotion', warns of the dangerous feelings you may be hiding beneath your normal smiling, helpful self. Appropriate anger or jealousy are perfectly healthy emotions, and are only destructive when they eat you away.

Earth

Fire

Lynne has a modern marriage in which she and her husband Jack have separate friends of both sexes and avoid questioning each other about their activities when they are apart. But recently one of Jack's female colleagues, Jan, has been through a traumatic relationship and Jack has been spending most of his evenings providing a shoulder to cry on. Twice recently he has let Lynne down when she needed him to come to a works dinner because Jan was upset and now he has said they can't go on holiday until Jan feels able to cope without him.

Lynne can see reason but she's put on half a stone and taken up smoking. Her Fire-Earth hexagram says that perhaps it is time for her to express her negative emotions and need for support, before her modern marriage becomes a modern divorce statistic.

Fire-Water gives the 'keeping up the momentum' hexagram. We've made the finishing post and all our efforts have paid off. Now comes the hard part — pushing on and not resting on our laurels.

Water

Fire

Callie got a place at university with apparently little effort and is now reaping the benefits of an active social life on a course with few other females. Her grades have been acceptable though not brilliant and now she has been asked to organise the first year review which will be staged a few days after the exams. It will cut down considerably on her revising time but Callie hopes she can 'busk' the exams and work harder next year.

Callie makes the Fire-Water hexagram and there she is at a top college having a great time and now the chance to organise the coveted review. On the other hand – perhaps she should put a little more effort into the mundane matters of work right now before her academic career goes off the boil.

Fire-Thunder is the 'peak achievement' hexagram. These special moments in life are very short, and tomorrow the world goes on its mundane way. So we should enjoy the good moments while we can.

Thunder

Fire

Connie has saved for many years to fulfil her ambition to sail on the QE2 and at last has just enough money for the trip. But her married son says it is a waste of money and she should buy herself a decent conservatory for her house where she can sit in the summer and which will add to the value of her property.

Connie's Fire-Thunder hexagram made her decide that she should go and enjoy her peak moment which will probably be just as wonderful as she imagined and let Mr Fuddy-Duddy son fret about the size of his inheritance.

**Fire-Tree is the hexagram of 'the forest fire'
or 'clearing the way'.** It may be that your
world is changing in a way you don't like. But
the destruction can clear away an old dead
part of our lives and leave room for new
growth.

Tree

Fire

Rosemary's husband has run off with a
younger woman after twenty years of marriage
leaving her alone at fifty, for they never had
children. He has agreed to support her financially and signed over to her the house which
she has always hated as it was his late
grandmother's and is like a Victorian
mausoleum.

Rosemary makes Fire-Tree. There is nothing to stop her throwing out all the heavy old
furniture and painting the walls white or red
or whatever she fancies. On the other hand
she could sell the house which she has never
felt is hers and buy a flat or another smaller
house that she does like.

Fire-Mountain — the 'hidden conflict'
hexagram, a volcano bubbling away inside
that could erupt at any time. However daunt-
ing, open those official envelopes or tackle

the mutterings at work or home now, before the situation gets out of control.

Mountain

Fire

Tanya, in her late thirties, is in the fast lane for promotion. Her long-standing partner, Lee, who comes from a large family has been trying to raise the issue of children for several years, but she has always said that children will come later. Recently they had a big argument over her refusal even to discuss children and Tanya went into work on Sunday to avoid the issue.

Her Fire-Mountain hexagram says the problem won't go away. So now is the time to sit down and be honest with her partner, to express her fears and feelings and see whether they can agree on a solution or to resolve their own future if they can't compromise.

Fire-Lake — the 'talking to deaf ears' hexagram has the sun reflected in the water. Try to understand why the other person has switched off — it's easy to blame ourselves but the others may be deliberately shutting themselves away.

Lake

Fire

Rhona's husband Daniel has recently been made redundant and has completely withdrawn into himself. Rhona has found herself becoming increasingly shrill and not supporting him as she would like to because she feels she just can't get through to him.

Her Fire-Lake hexagram may be telling her that for now she should stop trying to cheer him up and concentrate on her own problems thrown up by the redundancy. Daniel may even open up once she stops coaxing him as he may feel less pressurised.

WATER

The eight Water hexagrams talk about going with the flow and using any new opportunity, however unlikely or risky, to move forward rather than wait for an ideal opportunity to present itself.

Double Water — the 'taking a chance' hexagram occurs when an opportunity presents itself for radical change, not necessarily in location but in lifestyle or even attitude — it may be the only way out of present difficulties, and certainly worth the gamble.

Water

Water

Chloe feels stuck in a rut as manager of a small health centre. Though well-paid she has little contact with patients and after eight years dreads going to work. An old friend has offered her a job, not anywhere exotic, but helping to set up a play scheme in Glasgow for an international charity. If it goes well she may be able to transfer to another project anywhere from Bangladesh to Wigan. But the move does involve a drop in pay as well as giving up the comfortable flat over the health centre where she has lived since leaving school. Her new job description varies from demanding and challenging to exhausting. Should Chloe take a chance?

Chloe's Double-Water hexagram reflects some deep-seated need for change and challenge. She is stagnating while out there the unknown, dangerous and definitely exciting is waiting.

Water-Sky — the hexagram of 'doing without the approval of others'. Independence from the 'approvers' is necessary to fulfil our own dreams and not other people's.

Sky

Water

Glenys is in her early seventies but still is under the influence of big sister Glenda with whom she has shared a house since the death of her husband five years ago. Now Glenys has met Joe, a man of her own age she would like to marry, but her sister has taken a violent dislike to him because she says he is after Glenys's money. Sis is making it very difficult for Glenys to realise any of her capital. Joe says it doesn't matter — they can move into his mobile home and live on their pensions. Glenys is undecided because she has always relied on her sister, even during her marriage, for advice and approval.

Her Water-Sky hexagram suggests that now is the time to strike out away from her sister and take a chance on the new relationship. At seventy, chances for new happiness don't grow on every tree.

Water-Earth — the 'Nest Egg' hexagram. The water is contained in the dam (the earth) for when it is needed, and so it is important for women to build up a store of background skills and personal resources, even if they seem to have no immediate use.

Earth

Water

Cheryl is in her last year of university and was hoping to go on to take a higher degree. However, her boyfriend whom she has known since childhood and who works in his father's hardware shop says she's wasted enough time getting qualifications she'll never use and it's about time she comes home, gets married and works in the shop which they will inherit one day.

Her Water-Earth hexagram accurately reflects her own feelings. Eventually she settles on a compromise, not going on to more full-time study but enrolling for a part-time course at a local college.

Water-Fire — the 'damp squib' hexagram. Unlike Fire-Water, where the fire is heating the water above, the water below is putting out the fire. If you do really want change, you've got to accept it's all or nothing. But, if what you've got is what you want, stop fretting about what might have been.

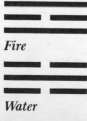

Fire

Water

Judith has always said that when the children left home she would leave her husband. But the last child went to college two years ago and every time she makes a plan to move out, something prevents her. Now her middle daughter has announced her engagement and Judith feels she shouldn't spoil her daughter's big day. But at each attempt to leave she gets herself steamed up and then her plans fizzle out, leaving her feeling worse than if she hadn't threatened to go.

Judith draws Water-Fire and perhaps the first question she should ask is does she really want to leave her husband or is it a desperate reaction to get some positive response from him? If she is serious she should leave regardless of how convenient it is for those close to her.

Water-Thunder — the 'clearing the air' hexagram when there's no point wasting time or energy in regrets. The important thing is 'what next?'. If it is time to move on, then it is important to see what led to the situation and how it can be avoided in future.

Thunder

Water

Janet has put up with her husband's affairs for twenty years but had always said this time is the last. Now the tell-tale signs are beginning again and after a terrible argument Janet has told Greg to get out and initiated an official separation. Greg has moved in with a friend but has sent a message he would like to come home and that he will give the other woman up. Should Janet take him back though for the first time in years she feels free of tension?

The Water-Thunder hexagram reflects the fact that she has delivered the death blow to a very sickly marriage. Now it is important for her to consider her own future. She may realise in her heart of hearts he will never change and use the impetus of the separation to begin a new life for herself.

Water-Tree — the hexagram of 'bridging the gap', whether between warring family members or at work. The Tree can act as a bridge over the water because the issue at stake is worthwhile.

Tree

Water

Stephanie's daughter, Jo, left home to live with her drop-out boyfriend when she became pregnant and her husband refused to have any more to do with his daughter. However, Stephanie has remained in touch and has sent money and been to see the baby. Now Jo's boyfriend has deserted her and Stephanie is anxious her daughter and grandchild should return home, at least for a time until she sorts her future out. But Stephanie's husband is adamant that Jo has made her bed and should lie on it while Jo is bitter at her father's rejection of the grandchild. Stephanie wonders whether to give up on the situation.

She makes the Water-Tree hexagram and so it seems she should continue to act as a bridge between the warring factions if only for the sake of her granddaughter.

Water-Mountain — the hexagram of 'going back to the source of the trouble'. The image is of the mountain spring from which the river rises, and most resentments start from a simple misunderstanding or off-handed response that can escalate into a full-blown war.

Mountain

Water

Sophie is in her late forties and hasn't spoken to her best friend Maxine for almost a year after a disagreement over the church concert. Maxine walked out in a huff and has avoided her friend ever since except to nod at church. Now Sophie's daughter is getting married and wants to invite Aunty Maxine, whom she has known since childhood. But Sophie says that their friendship is very definitely over and Maxine's presence would ruin the whole day.

Sophie's Water-Mountain hexagram suggests that it may be time to examine the source of the coldness and see if such a trivial quarrel can't be overcome at least for the sake of her daughter.

Water-Lake — the hexagram of feeling drained or 'empty milk bottle' hexagram. For all the water has drained from the lake and so, for now, you have no inner resources left. It is time for you to rest and call on some of those favours you're owed.

Lake

Water

Lorraine is unofficial agony aunt to colleagues, friends and family alike as well as providing room service to the world and her family. Now Lorraine is feeling constantly ill and exhausted but can't sleep for worrying about everyone else.

The Water-Lake hexagram shows she is running on empty and needs to nurture herself and call on a few of the able-bodied, if emotionally fragile individuals around her. A few days in bed for starters would perhaps alert everyone that the ship is sinking and when those half-hearted offers of help arrive she should galvanise the volunteers into action.

THUNDER

The Thunder hexagrams talk about sudden changes to the status quo that you initiate when you feel that you are being unfairly treated.

Double Thunder — the 'straw that broke the camel's back' hexagram occurs when a long-standing injustice suddenly becomes intolerable. So be aware of the signs of your own rising irritation.

Thunder

Thunder

Marcia has spent five years taking care of her elderly mother who refuses any welfare provision, such as meals on wheels or day care, insisting that it is Marcia's place to take care of her. Now Marcia has the opportunity to accompany her husband on an all-expenses-paid, month-long business trip. However, the old lady refuses to accept any alternative care and says she will starve if Marcia leaves her.

Marcia draws Double-Thunder which suggests that it is time to stop the old lady's emotional blackmail and Marcia should go calmly ahead with her holiday plans, alerting the relevant agencies in the knowledge that her mother's strong sense of self-preservation will ensure she will accept the help offered if there is no alternative.

Thunder-Sky — the hexagram of 'seizing the opportunity'. If we can take advantage of the highs in our life, the times when we do feel energetic and positive, then we have something in store for times when we are tired and run down.

Sky

Thunder

Lizzie is in her late twenties and unattached. She has been offered the chance to go on an intensive language course paid for by her firm that will enable her to apply for jobs at branches abroad. But she is part of a very close-knit group of friends who are pressuring her to turn down the opportunity as it will interfere with their holiday plans for the summer.

Her Thunder-Sky hexagram suggests that, now is the time in her life when she is free of commitments and can make a leap forward in her career. If she passes up the chance now it may not come again.

Thunder-Earth — 'the turning point' or 'awakening' hexagram. When life collapses about our ears, we need to rest physically and emotionally until life stirs again. This hexagram tells us that it is time to move cautiously into the sunlight.

Earth

Thunder

Maureen's first child was stillborn but she refused to discuss her loss or to contemplate another child. A year has passed and she has started going along to a group of similarly bereaved women and for the first time has been able to share her experiences with her husband and to realise how he too has suffered. He has asked her if she will consider having another child when she is ready.

When she draws Thunder-Earth, Maureen admits to herself that although she can never replace the child she has lost, she is almost ready to try again for a child.

Thunder-Fire — the 'supreme effort' hexagram. The Thunder is the more powerful element in this storm. Sometimes it is necessary to make one mighty push to finish an essential piece of work or save a relationship.

Fire

Thunder

Amy is moving to Canada with her husband, Jack. Her parents are not speaking to her because of a violent quarrel with him and didn't even make contact when Amy's son was born. Jack says there is no point in telling them about the move but Amy fears she may not see her father again since he has a serious heart condition.

Her Thunder-Fire hexagram suggests she should make one last supreme effort with her parents, perhaps going to see them so that the family does not part, perhaps for the last time in anger.

Thunder-Water — the new direction or 'shooting the rapids' hexagram. The power of the thunder pushes the water in an entirely different direction after difficulties have blocked a path.

Water

Thunder

Sue has been renting her flat with two friends for five years but the landlord is putting up the rent out of the tenants' reach and a mortgage on a similar property is out of the question. All efforts to rent another flat have drawn a blank. Suddenly a derelict cottage five miles out of town has come on to the market and they could just afford it with loans from family. But it will need a great deal of effort and money to restore the crumbling heap into a dream home. The others are keen but Sue hesitates.

She draws the Thunder-Water hexagram. The cottage is a considerable gamble. But since homelessness beckons, it might be time to make the jump into the property market despite the difficulties.

Thunder-Tree — the hexagram of 'changing our perception'. The tree is above the thunder and its roots are shaken like our old beliefs, which may have seemed true simply because they were untested.

Tree

Thunder

Eva believed she was free from racial prejudice. But when her son brought home a West Indian nurse and announced they were getting married Eva flipped. Now her son refuses to speak to her.

She draws the Thunder-Tree hexagram and realises that her own liberated attitudes were based on beliefs that had never been tested. So now she needs to look at her real fears about the situation and to explain her outburst to her son who can't understand his mother's apparent about-face from her liberal principles.

Thunder-Mountain — the 'input' hexagram, represents the time when the seeds have been scattered by the Thunder and need time and nurturing to reach fruition.

Mountain

Thunder

Sally has sold some of the pottery she has made and would like to make a full-time career as a potter instead of teaching crafts at the local technical college. She is finding the effort of trying to hold down two jobs as well as care for a family a great strain. Should she abandon her dream and stick to teaching?

Her Thunder-Mountain doesn't offer any easy solutions. She needs to carry on nourishing those seeds of her dream though she is finding it very hard slog. But not to work towards her dream is to lose an important part of herself so the Ching says 'keep at it'.

Thunder-Lake — the hexagram of 'inner strength' because of the thunder deep in the lake. To strengthen our inner resources and creativity we need to withdraw for a time from the frantic round of activities with which we cram our days.

Lake

Thunder

Shirley, a succesful nursing sister, is very interested in a holistic approach to illness and has been asked to spend her holidays lecturing on the subject. She had planned to spend the month's leave she was owed walking around the Lake District alone but she is fired with enthusiasm for her subject. However, after her break she is taking up a new even more demanding post that will give her little free time.

Shirley's Thunder-Lake suggests that she should think very carefully before giving up her holiday. In a job that is spiritually rewarding as well as mentally and physically demanding it is casy to overlook the need for solitude and rest.

TREE

The eight Tree hexagrams represent the need to approach change slowly step by step, while refusing to be discouraged or dissuaded.

Double Tree, — the hexagram of 'persistence', is often met when a woman is trying to institute change but seems blocked at every turn. These blockages can be overcome, given persistence and a belief that the goal being worked for is worthwhile.

Tree

Tree

Louise was almost at the end of a long degree course she had taken in her spare time at a local college while bringing up children when her husband Roger broke the news that he was being transferred to the other end of the country almost immediately. Roger couldn't understand Louise's reluctance to up sticks and pack and accused her of putting her stupid degree course before the family's happiness. Louise says she's only got four months to go before her finals and wants to stay put till then.

Her Double-Tree suggests that she should stick to her guns and let her husband go ahead and come back at weekends, until after her exams when she and the family can join him. It certainly won't be easy but if Louise gives up years of work at the last fence, she might always regret it and perhaps end up resenting her husband.

Tree-Sky — the hexagram of 'aiming high' points out that many women don't try to compete for fear of being considered unfeminine. But if you want to aim high, whether for personal recognition or in the world of work, be bold and go straight for it.

Sky

Tree

Moira is the only girl doing Computer Studies A Level at school and the male students are subtly undermining her. She is hoping to take a degree in Computer Studies but lately she has been getting very rattled in class. Her male teacher is supportive on the surface but takes any opportunity to let the boys know it's all lads together.

Moira makes the Tree-Sky hexagram and so should aim high, despite the prejudice. She needs to set her sights on a good A level which is her most potent weapon against those who feel threatened by her abilities.

Tree-Earth — the hexagram of starting from where you are, not where you'd like to be. The ideal situation is rare but each step taken is a step forward, however small.

Earth

Tree

Viv is in her early fifties and caring for her elderly father at home, having given up a successful career and flat because she felt her father could no longer be alone. The days stretch emptily before her. Viv has been invited to a carers' club that is attached to the Day Care Centre her father attends two days a week.

She makes the Tree-Earth hexagram and there isn't a lot on offer on her horizon apart from the club. It may not seem ideal but at least it's a step towards keeping in touch with the outside world. And Viv may find people like herself who have given up an interesting lives to care for ailing relatives and who can give her at least some stimulation for those few hours away from duty. They could even make a run for the nearest wine bar when the tea is handed out.

Tree-Fire — the hexagram of 'the life cycle', for the wood must burn to give substance to the fire, and so becomes ash to return to the earth. We have to give up one stage of life to begin another, though sometimes there is real pain and loss involved.

Fire

Tree

Peggy's only daughter Tracey is married but comes home every time she and her husband Don have a quarrel over even the most trivial matter. There is bad feeling with Don because he says that Peggy babies Tracey and that unless she grows up he won't be around next time she runs back to Mum.

Peggy makes the Tree-Fire hexagram and whatever the rights and wrongs of the situation decides that Tracey coming back to Mum at the first sign of trouble clearly isn't helping the couple to resolve their difficulties. So perhaps Peggy needs to push her baby bird out of the nest for her own sake.

Tree-Water — the Well. In the Well of Knowledge inside you, your intuition can provide an answer to your dilemma.

Water

Tree

Charlotte has left a violent husband and now has met a man who seems gentle, caring and understanding. He has suggested that he moves into her council flat with her and her young child. However recently they attended a wedding and Frank got very drunk. Afterwards there was a quarrel and he hit her. However he was immediately remorseful and has promised never to touch alcohol again.

Charlotte draws the Tree-Water hexagram which suggests she should listen to her own inner wisdom that is warning her against letting history repeat itself. It may be the relationship needs to develop much more slowly before Frank moves in — if ever.

Tree-Thunder — the hexagram of 'resisting outside pressures'. You may be being browbeaten and worn down to give up your own needs, but whether it's a haranguing boss or a complaining elderly mother, giving in to them only makes future attacks more likely and easy.

Thunder

Tree

Lorraine has three adolescent children who would make the Mafia appear like Cub Scouts. The eldest has just left school but hasn't got a job and the younger two truant regularly and slam round the house and argue loudly if she doesn't subsidise them. Her husband, a long-distance lorry driver, tends to clout them round the ear when he is home and then slam out to the pub to get a bit of peace. Lorraine is desperate to make ends meet out of her wages as a supervisor in the local supermarket, but fears the boys will, as they threaten, steal money if she doesn't give it to them.

She draws the Tree-Thunder hexagram and perhaps it's time to call their bluff, decide what she can afford and what they deserve in terms of input to the household and stick to her guns.

Tree-Mountain — the hexagram of 'going your own way'. It may make you a loner at times, but unless we live life on our own terms, we can end up feeling very empty, even if others consider we are successful.

Mountain

Tree

Mary is in her twenties, lives in a small terraced cottage by the sea left to her by her mother and makes a modest living as a freelance photographer. She recently won a major competition for one of her pictures and has been offered a job on a London newspaper. But Mary is very happy and is reluctant to give up and leave her present way of life to live in the city which she hates.

Her Tree-Mountain hexagram indicates she should do whatever it is that makes her happy, whether or not it conforms with other people's definitions of success.

Tree-Lake — the 'feeling overwhelmed' hexagram. You can't please everyone; and you feel as though you are drowning. So wait for the floods to go down. Deal only with life and death issues and, for the rest, either refuse or delay any immediate action on your part.

Lake

Tree

Maxine is Union treasurer at work and tends to be the unofficial counsellor for the problems of the women members. Now she has been asked to take on the position as Women's Rep for the County which willmean she will tackle problems on an official and confrontational basis rather than the present informal basis. Maxine feels that she is being used as a pawn for other people and feels totally overwhelmed and wishes she'd never got involved.

Her Tree-Lake hexagram confirms that she is being overwhelmed by conflicting demands, not least her own need to keep on good terms with her bosses as well as represent her fellow members. Maxine can then go on with her excellent informal approach to women's issues at work.

MOUNTAIN

The Mountain hexagrams talk about achieving peace and inner harmony by moving away from petty quarrels and the need for the approval of others, and clearly marking your own personal boundaries.

Double Mountain — the 'fighting for space' hexagram often appears when your needs have been submerged in those around you. Start to express your wishes, needs and preferences if you are not to be swamped.

Mountain

Mountain

Abigail, a teacher in her early twenties, is in the middle of her first intense love affair and she and Steve have moved into a flat together. Over the past few months they have dropped most of their friends and since Steve has lost contact with his family, he has discouraged

Abigail from seeing her parents to whom she had been very close. Now Abigail's mother has offered her the chance to spend three weeks in Australia with her grandmother, who has not been well and has sent the fare for her daughter and grandaughter to see her for perhaps the last time.

Abigail is torn. She really wants to see her grandma again but feels disloyal to Steve who can't go and says she can't either.

Her Double-Mountain hexagram suggests that perhaps she has allowed herself to become too submerged in her new relationship. Perhaps she should make a stand now before the two hearts beating as one becomes too rigid a pattern.

Mountain-Sky — the hexagram of 'drawing the line' marks the point at which you find yourself withdrawing either physically or emotionally. But this can reveal a whole new range of possibilities and extra energy once you stop banging your head against a brick wall.

Sky

Mountain

Cathy spends much of her energy worrying about her adolescent son who has got in with a bad crowd and has started truanting from school. Her husband has no patience with the boy and she is constantly covering the boy's tracks and bribing him when his father upsets him and he threatens to go on the streets. She has started to have blackouts but the doctor says there is no physical reason for her illness.

Cathy's Mountain-Sky indicates that her peace-keeping role is wrecking her own well-being. She needs to expose both combatants to the consequences of their actions and force her husband and the school to sort out the truanting.

Mountain-Earth — the hexagram of 'hidden ambitions' often appears when a woman's dreams are submerged by the needs of others. It reminds us that it is essential to hold the dream and, where possible, to prepare for the day you can climb that mountain.

Earth

Mountain

Margaret has been a health visitor for many years, but though she enjoys her work immensely, has always wanted to write a book on castles in her native Scotland. Her aunt has left her a small cottage on the Borders and though it will be a struggle to maintain it and her London flat on her present salary, she would love to use it as a base to research her book when she retires.

Mountain-Earth reminds her of her hidden ambition. It may be a financial struggle right now but the cottage will give her a base for holidays over the next few years so she can begin in a modest way to study her interest. Even if she doesn't get her book published she can look forward to the pleasure of researching and writing it.

Mountain-Fire — the 'moving on' hexagram, may appear when you've realised that the current situation, though exciting, will quickly burn out. So prepare to move on while the situation is still alive, rather than linger in the ashes of regret.

Fire

Mountain

Marion has met the man of her dreams, rich, handsome and exciting and she is enjoying life in the fast lane, which makes a change from the surburban insurance office and childhood sweetheart that, until now have formed the limits of her world. Carl has asked her to go away into the sunset with him — crewing on a yacht to the West Indies to find their paradise.

Mountain-Fire confirms her suppressed fear that although the fire of love may be burning very fiercely at the moment it may not last that long. Should she go back to her old ways? The hexagram is about moving on, so perhaps this is a chance for Marion to make positive plans about her own future. Her insurance firm does have a system for transferring between offices, so this might be the time for Marion to get out her map and start moving.

Mountain-Water — is the hexagram of '**being obstructed**' but not by an insurmountable object. Follow the stillness in the mountain and proceed cautiously. Is there a way round the obstacle? If you must leap, then do look first — and try to have a safety net.

Water

Mountain

Hetty is in her late fifties and her company has been taken over by a multi-national with orders to boost profits. Hetty can already see the new ruthless approach is jeopardising the former happy atmosphere between staff and customers and setting former colleagues at each other's throats. She fears her only option is to resign. But it is doubtful even with her experience she would find a new job at her age.

Her Mountain-Water reflects the pretty hefty obstacle in her path. But it counsels the caution she knows deep in her heart is necessary. Is there any alternative to resigning? Can her approach to her colleagues and customers temper the new broom that may be sweeping keen but not clean?

Mountain-Thunder — the 'hot air' hexagram, warns that while you may think you are expressing your discontent pretty loudly, it is being ignored. Direct the thunder at the perpetrator of the injustice and make definite demands in a firm but not over-the-top manner.

Thunder

Mountain

Maria, like many middle-aged family women, struggles to juggle job and home and gets very little practical help from her husband or teenage daughter. Maria has yelled, nagged and moaned but her family just laugh. Maria is eaten up with resentment which is souring the good bit of the relationships.

Mountain-Thunder shows her what she knows but hasn't accepted: that her protests are getting nowhere fast. So it's time to change tactics and make a list of what she is prepared to do around the house and then draw up a rota for the other jobs and stick to it. Even to the extent of eating out and letting the others fend for themselves.

Mountain-Tree — the hexagram of 'standing alone' says that while it takes a lot of courage to swim against the tide, it is important to be what we feel is right for us. Though it may seem a lonely hexagram, it can ultimately be a very fulfilling one.

Tree

Mountain

Blair gave up work as a journalist three months ago to care for her new baby full-time and has found herself swept into a new world of coffee mornings and mother and baby groups. But she is starting to dread the social gatherings as she feels she doesn't get enough time alone, either with the baby, or to pursue her fiction writing which she had hoped to develop while she was at home.

Mountain-Tree says it is OK to opt out and pursue a different course if that is right for her. Though the path to success may be slow and difficult nevertheless she should not feel guilty about going it alone.

Mountain-Lake — the hexagram of 'responding to inner needs'. If the inner and outer harmonies are balanced, you can whistle and sing your way along the stoniest path. But this happiness depends on *your* needs, not acting out roles others set for you.

Lake

Mountain

Dawn is in her thirties and is married to a vicar who expects her to act as unofficial parish worker and back-up service. But she hates her parish duties and now the children are at school she would like to return to full-time teaching. But Don fears this will mean she neglects her parish duties. Dawn is torn between her desire to make a life for herself in a field she loves and keep her husband happy which means continuing the lie.

Her Mountian-Lake hexagram suggests that however difficult, unless Dawn follows her own path then she won't feel happy inside and that she won't be able to keep up the pretence forever.

LAKE

The Lake hexagrams talk about the happiness that comes from within ourselves and not others, and can appear when our lives are so packed with activity that we lose touch with ourselves and start to feel empty.

Double Lake — the 'automatic pilot' hexagram may be a signal to slow down and take the phone off the hook. We may find perhaps that the life we are leading isn't what we need to find happiness.

Lake

Lake

Maggie runs aerobic classes in the evening as well as holding down a part-time job and running a home. No one has ever heard Maggie utter a cross word or refuse to help. But three or four times during the last month she has had minor accidents in the kitchen and had to cancel her last aerobics class because she had a migraine — something she has never done before.

Double-Lake warns her that her body is saying slow down and give yourself time to get back in touch with yourself.

Lake-Sky — the hexagram of 'inner creativity', says that however successful you may be in the outside world, you have come to realise that what you feel inside is not finding expression.

Sky

Lake

Helen is a divorced successful businesswoman in her fifties who travels around Britain selling her firm's products and maps out her life down to the last squash game or time with her grown-up daughter. Now her daughter is pregnant without a permanent partner and Helen feels that she wants to get to know the baby in a way she never had time to do with her own child. But this would be at odds with her plans to accept a job as manager of a firm in Geneva.

Helen's Lake-Sky hexagram may suggest that her creative power of mothering has been pushed to one side in the pursuit of her own career. However with her daughter's pregnancy there is a place for inner creativity in her life if she really does want to slow down to be with her daughter and grandchild.

Lake-Earth — the 'back to grass roots' hexagram can appear when life has swept you along a path you aren't entirely happy with. Time to look back to find the goals you had when you started out.

Earth

Lake

Jo is working for her A levels and is set to study botany at university at her parents' insistence. However she finds formal study an incredible strain. What she really wants to do is to work in her uncle's garden centre and learn the business on a practical level. Her parents say she must complete a degree first.

She draws Lake-Earth which indicates that although the degree would seem a better foundation for a career. It may be that Jo will find happiness in the less-high powered approach. Ultimately if Jo goes to university purely to please her parents, she is accepting their definition of success and may even fail.

Lake-Fire — the 'inner voice' hexagram. Life may well have seemed a slog, but look around, and suddenly there seems a point to it all. You can see that you are on course for real happiness.

Fire

Lake

Meg has been training as an aromatherapist in her spare time though her family and colleagues at work have been telling her she is wasting her time learning to be a glorified beautician instead of concentrating on her banking exams which will guarantee promotion.

She was on the point of giving up when she drew the Lake-Fire hexagram. This brought to mind an acquaintance who was suffering from migraines and had asked her for advice. Meg's new found expertise had dramatically improved the woman's condition. Meg knows she still has a way to go to qualify but now she sees that her future career not only has a point but that she does have the necessary skills within her to make the grade.

Lake-Water — the 'batten down the hatches' hexagram. You are in danger of overflowing with all those demands for your time and energy raining down. You can't satisfy them all so you might as well please yourself.

Water

Lake

Noelene has got her golden wedding party to organise and already she's hit snags. Her folks hate his family even after all these years and they are demanding that choices are made. People are demanding hotel accommodation overnight and her own children are vying for top position on the high table. The teenage grandchildren refuse to come unless there's a disco and gran says she'll boycott the occasion if the young people insist on loud music. Noelene has a permanent headache and her husband says he'd sooner not bother.

Her Lake-Water hexagram sugessts that it's not worth the hassle. If Noelene does want to mark her Golden Wedding, why not use the money on a really nice holiday for the only two people really involved, herself and her husband? As for the warring relatives, Noelene can send them a postcard.

Lake-Thunder — the 'ruffled feathers' hexagram can warn you when you are under attack, and tell you to let things settle down before you plan your response. When you are calm, decide whether it's worth getting steamed up or better to concentrate on more positive matters.

Thunder

Lake

Samantha has been married for six months and is finding it hard to get on with her new sister-in-law, Sonia, who was very close to her brother and now makes every possible attempt to exclude Samantha or put her down. At a family party, Sonia insisted on getting out the photos of her brother with his former girlfriends and to point out he married Sam on the rebound from a broken engagement. Derek sees nothing wrong in his sister's behaviour but Samantha has written her sister-in-law a long letter pouring out all the resentment. She is carrying it round in her bag. Should she post it?

The Lake-Thunder hexagram warns her to wait until she has cooled down and then consider whether or not she would be giving her sister-in-law ammunition to use at a future date when the original grievance is forgotten. It might be better to ignore Sonia's attempts at trouble-making and make subtle attempts to steer her husband into spending less time with his family.

Lake-Tree the 'stand by your principles' hexagram can provide support when you are wavering about acting over some injustice. It reminds us how important it is for a woman to draw the line at what she sees is unfair.

Tree

Lake

Sheila works in a charity shop two days a week and local stores sometimes hand on their seconds to help swell the profits. However the charity workers themselves tend to cream off the best goods and make only a nominal donation. The general public are left with the cast-offs that no one wants and the shop is not making money. Should Sheila speak out at the next meeting even though she might upset a lot of people she is very close to?

The Lake-Tree hexagram suggests that she may find it impossible to stay silent at the meeting. Her options are to approach a senior member of the organisation in confidence so the matter can be broached by another source, to leave the shop or to speak out. Clearly valuable sources of funding are being diverted so she can't just ignore the issue and carry on.

Lake-Mountain — the 'future investment' hexagram. We may have to give up something that is important to us right now in order to build for a future that seems remote. However painful the sacrifice, it promises hope for the future.

Mountain

Lake

Sandra plays classical guitar in her spare time and has performed semi-professionally during the evenings. Now she is pregnant and realises that she will have to curtail her musical activities in order to fit in work and family commitments. Despite desperately wanting a child, she feels very resentful that her performing days are numbered.

Sandra makes the Lake-Mountain hexagram and it would be foolish to pretend she can have it all. But playing her guitar can still be an important part of her life and, as well as giving her child immense pleasure and keeping her in practice for when she can return to the stage, she has the chance of bringing up her child to appreciate and perhaps play music. That must be a pretty important investment in the future.

Summary

Yang ——, the unbroken line is the masculine, creative, challenging, logical side that, in the right dose, makes woman get up and go without trampling all over others.

Yang

Yin — — is the darker, receptive, accepting, intuitive side of the woman (and man) that is essential for any nurturing role, whether of ourselves, our children, parents, friends or the world in general.

Yin

The Trigrams

The three in a row **'all the same'** trigrams.

Three *yangs* (unbroken lines) stand for:

Pure *yang* is the creative burst of energy for a new venture or a leap forward, using your head rather than your heart.

Sky

Three yins (broken lines) stand for:

Pure *yin,* the Earth, is the receptive, intuitive, caring aspect that is central to a woman's being. Just don't get too loaded down with other people's emotional shopping.

Earth

In the **'Sandwich Trigrams'** the middle line is sandwiched by two opposites.

Fire

Two yangs (unbroken lines) sandwiching a *yin* (broken line) stand for;

This is the flickering fire in the grate, two loads of oomph *(yang)* fuelled by the earth (the middle line). Fire is the communication trigram, putting that energy and those good ideas into practice with a good solid basis, the earthing of the creative spark.

Water

Two *yins* sandwiching a *yang*, like a river moving between its earthy (broken) and changing banks stand for:

Water involves going with the flow and accepting any opportunities that arise regardless of the apparent difficulty or danger.

The 'bottom line' or movement trigrams.

Thunder

Thunder, the trigram of deliberate sudden change. The single powerful *yang* (unbroken line at the bottom) rising from the earth and splitting the sky into two broken lines.

Thunder is the sudden decision that enough is enough that makes a woman speak out and shocks those around who have found the status quo an easy ride.

Tree

Tree, the trigram of gradual change. The single *yin* pushes its way from the earth (broken line) and has to inch its way upwards through the obstacles ahead and above, that seek to stifle its growth — remember the glass ceiling that inhibits progress upwards.

The Tree represents a woman's personal growth inch by inch and the gentle persistence that is her greatest strength against all the storms that seek to uproot her or divert her from her path.

The trigrams of 'keeping the lid on', and of stillness are determined by their top line.

Mountain is two lots of earth (broken lines) piled up, giving a peak, a single unbroken line that touches the sky.

Mountain

Mountain represents moving away from disruption, stepping out of the firing line, ceasing to try to be all things to all men, and marking your own limits as a way to a personal harmony.

Lake is the reversed mountain with the earth (broken line at the top) pushing the peaks downwards to form an indentation for the lake.

Lake

Lake, not surprisingly, represents the happiness that lies in looking to our inner resources and taking a rest from the world's non-stop roadshow, however enjoyable.

The Hexagrams

Hexagrams are two trigrams one on top of the other to give six lines. We still read from the bottom up, so the hexagram is called by the name of the bottom trigram followed by the name of the top one. However, we read the positions of the trigrams in the usual way ie, the trigram that is physically the top one is regarded as being above when we create a picture in our mind.

Remember the tree underneath the lake because the Tree was the bottom trigram and the Lake the top (though we call it Tree-Lake).

Make the first trigram by taking three stones and placing them one on top of the other, as usual without looking which face is uppermost. Read what this trigram says, if you feel it helps you to see the hexagram as two distinct parts. The first trigram goes at the bottom.

Now form the second trigram on top of the first. Identify this one, then see what the two ideas together seem to be saying. See the hexagram as a picture, especially noting the positions of the elements in relation to each other.

If you can't see how the two trigrams relate, either have a look at my mini-definitions or read them separately, as two parts of a story, and see how the two aspects address your present situation. If the ideas don't naturally combine, they will in time.

You may still find it useful to do trigram readings with or without change lines, and though hexagrams do give a more detailed picture of the situation, if you can't make head nor tail of them, your trigram readings are quite adequate.

The Change Lines

There's nothing complicated about a change line in a trigram or hexagram. If it's a *yang* change line (or *old yang*) then it looks like the London Underground sign —0—.

If it's a *yin* change *(old yin)* then it is marked as a cross between the two broken lines —×—.

Use your new second set of twelve change stones to make a changing trigram (if you end up with one with no change lines, this indicates that you're going through a very stable period).

Read your trigram as usual, ignoring whether the *yin* and *yang* lines are changing or not and identify the trigram element.

Count your change lines: this will give you an idea of how rapidly change might occur — the more change lines, the faster the change.

Then turn over each one of the changing lines (leave the plain *yins* and *yangs* in place in the original trigram) and you'll see that you've got a new second trigram which tells you what's brewing.

Your Personal
I Ching Diary

Date	Reading

Your Personal I Ching Diary

Date	Reading

Your Personal I Ching Diary

Date	Reading

Your Personal I Ching Diary

Date	Reading

Your Personal
I Ching Diary

Date	Reading

Your Personal
I Ching Diary

Date	Reading